Thinking Beyond Sectors for Sustainable Development

Edited by
Jeff Waage and Christopher Yap

]u[

ubiquity press
London

Published by
Ubiquity Press Ltd.
Gordon House
29 Gordon Square
London WC1H 0PP
www.ubiquitypress.com

Text © The Authors 2015

First published 2015

Cover Image: Christopher T Cooper
Savanna and a dirt road
http://commons.wikimedia.org/
Used under CC-BY 3.0 license

ISBN (Paperback): 978-1-909188-42-6
ISBN (PDF): 978-1-909188-43-3
ISBN (EPUB): 978-1-909188-44-0
ISBN (Kindle): 978-1-909188-45-7

DOI: http://dx.doi.org/10.5334/bao

Suggested citation:
Waage, J. and Yap, C. (eds.) 2015. *Thinking Beyond Sectors for Sustainable
Development*. London: Ubiquity Press. DOI: http://dx.doi.org/10.5334/bao

To read the online open access version of this
book, either visit http://dx.doi.org/10.5334/bao
or scan this QR code with your mobile device:

Contents

Acknowledgements v

Contributing institutions v

Statement vi

How this book came about vii

Foreword ix

Contributors xv

Part I: Perspectives on the Post-2015 Sustainable Development Agenda 1

Biodiversity and ecosystems 3

Climate and climate change 11

Urbanisation and urban poverty reduction in low- and middle-income countries 19

Human health 29

Population growth 37

Agriculture and food 45

Education, information, and knowledge 51

Governance and institutions 63

Part II: Thinking Beyond Sectors 77

Governing Sustainable Development Goals: interactions, infrastructures, and institutions 79

Case study on sexual and reproductive health and
education: reflections on interlinkage and governance   89

Appendix: Millennium Development Goals and Targets   109

Acknowledgements

This project was only possible due to the commitment of the large, multidisciplinary group of academics and researchers across the Bloomsbury Colleges at the University of London. In addition to the team that has collaborated to produce this volume, we would like to thank all the contributors to the project over its 18-month lifespan, whose ideas have helped to shape our response to developments in the international post-2015 agenda, and shaped a new space for interdisciplinary discussion and collaboration.

We are very thankful to University College London Grand Challenges for supporting this project and particularly to Helen Hopkins, Sarah Chaytor, and Kate Hoyland for their invaluable inputs and endless patience. We are also very grateful to Sam Mardell and Anna Marry at the London International Development Centre for their constant support and assistance through every stage of the project.

Contributing institutions

Statement

As we move from the era of the Millennium Development Goals to the Sustainable Development Goals it is important to consider how development agendas are set, the progress that has been made over the past 15 years, and how current debates are shaping global development efforts for the next 15 years.

This book was produced as part of a University College London-London International Development Centre research collaboration entitled *Thinking Beyond Sectors for Sustainable Development*. The aim of the book is to provide a concise introduction to debates in a number of vital development sectors, review progress made in each sector, and consider how looking beyond sectors might open new opportunities for inclusive, sustainable development.

Each chapter in this book was produced collaboratively by academics from a wide number of disciplines. As such, it represents a truly interdisciplinary and inter-sectoral effort, of the kind that will be necessary for the successful development and implementation of future international development goals.

How this book came about

Thinking Beyond Sectors for Sustainable Development began in spring 2013 when a group of London-based academics gathered to discuss the emerging discourse around the Sustainable Development Goals. The group comprised researchers from a wide range of disciplines across six London colleges: University College London and the group of Bloomsbury Colleges which together support the London International Development Centre, comprised of the London School of Hygiene and Tropical Medicine, Birkbeck College, School of Oriental and African Studies, Royal Veterinary College, and the Institute of Education (now the University College London Institute of Education).

Many of the researchers had been involved with earlier interdisciplinary analyses of the Millennium Development Goals, either through a University College London project supported by the interfaculty Grand Challenges programme, or through a project supported by the London International Development Centre. Both of these projects were published independently as Lancet Commissions.

An initial meeting of over 30 researchers from the Colleges mentioned above considered the broad development landscape and the way in which different post-2015 development expectations might interact, both positively and negatively. A number of development areas were identified on the basis of expertise in the Colleges and likely future development goals, guided by the outputs of the High-Level Panel on Post-2015 Sustainable Development.

For each sector, a small group of experts prepared summaries on the Millennium Development Goals experience, current debate on goal setting in that area, and likely interaction between that and other development targets. Summaries were developed on the areas of human health, climate and climate change, agriculture and food, population growth, governance and institutions, biodiversity and ecosystems, and urbanisation and urban poverty. Each was written by disciplinary experts in a way that allowed experts in other disciplines to quickly grasp the key issues. From this analysis, project participants created a matrix of potential interactions between different development goals. Some of these links proved obvious, such as the link between agricultural and environmental goals, but others were more subtle.

The project then moved to an intense interdisciplinary phase, with a workshop in March 2014 to explore the nature of interactions and the potential implications for global development. This workshop explored different clusters of goals and their potential interactions. While participants entered this workshop thinking about how to design targets and indicators that reflected interactions between goals, they concluded that there was a more important and less well-researched problem to address: how would such a diverse set of goals and interactions be effectively governed and delivered?

With this new emphasis on governance, several working groups were established to consider the challenge of governing particular clusters of goals and their interaction as a basis for developing a broader understanding. Three clusters were selected: agriculture-environment-climate change; energy-climate change-water; and health-population-education.

These working groups all produced reports for a workshop, where it was discovered that issues of interactions and governance in some clusters appeared much more tractable than in others. Working together, a pattern emerged: certain kinds of goals had similar intended outcomes, governance structures, and relations with other kinds of goals. This new understanding was developed into a conceptual model that identifies the opportunities and challenges for governance of future development goals. This new framework and perspective has emerged as the key output of this collaborative project.

This volume reflects this two-stage project. The first part of the book is a set of chapters based on disciplinary reflections prepared by groups of academics. The second part of the book develops an interdisciplinary approach and creates a framework for thinking beyond sectors, illustrated with a case study.

Foreword

Jeff Waage and Christopher Yap

The post-2015 development agenda and the Sustainable Development Goals (SDGs) represent a monumental opportunity and a challenge for policy makers, national and local governments, multilateral and bilateral agencies, and civil society around the world.

International cooperation towards global development has existed in a variety of forms for decades. Towards the end of the last century, a number of sectoral development initiatives began to set time-bound targets and goals. The establishment of the eight Millennium Development Goals (MDGs) in 2000 brought many of these initiatives together, and added more goals in new areas. It represented a paradigm shift in the way that global development efforts were coordinated and many governments in the global North and South made commitments to their achievement. The goals have framed and, to a large extent, defined development agendas for the past 15 years.[1]

As we approach 2015, it is clear that substantial progress has been made towards many MDGs, and some will be achieved. Between 2000 and 2015, the number of people living in extreme poverty has reduced by half, and the proportion of people without access to an improved drinking water source has also halved. Governments are also on target for reducing malaria and tuberculosis, and substantial progress has been made towards eliminating gender disparity in primary education. Other positive outcomes of the MDG process have been the improved coordination of development effort and investment, and the introduction, through goal targets and indicators, of a culture of measurement in international development programmes.

However, the Millennium Development agenda also had many shortcomings, in addition to falling short of targets in a number of cases. While the establishment of specific targets and indicators accelerated and focused efforts, achievements sometimes did not deliver what was intended. For instance, the goal to achieve universal primary education has made much progress in increasing enrolment in primary education in developing regions from 82 per cent in 1999 to 90 per cent in 2010, but there are concerns that the quality of

---

[1] For a full list of the Millennium Development Goals please see the Appendix.

learning has suffered. The goals also encountered problems of equity, with governments logically improving conditions for those most easy to reach, sometimes leaving the situation for the most marginalised unchanged. The goals were very specific and 'vertical' in their execution by different development communities. Moreover, champions of these goals failed to consider important interactions between development efforts and left many gaps. And, of course, development priorities changed over the 15 years. For instance, environmental issues, most notably climate change, have become much more central. These were very poorly represented in the initial goals, with vague targets reflecting a lack of political commitment in this area.

As 2015 approached, the United Nations began to work on the successor to the Millennium Development Goals. This process was strongly influenced by the view of many governments that any future goals should be 'goals for all' and address not only poverty reduction, the challenge in many poor countries, but sustainability, a problem shared by all. The Rio+20 United Nations Conference on Sustainable Development, held in Brazil in 2012, was to prove very influential in the development of the successors to the Millennium Development Goals.

The 1987 United Nations report *Our Common Future* (often referred to as the Brundtland Report) defines sustainable development in the following way:

> 'Humanity has the ability to make development sustainable to ensure that it meets the needs of the present without compromising the ability of future generations to meet their own needs. The concept of sustainable development does imply limits - not absolute limits but limitations imposed by the present state of technology and social organization on environmental resources and by the ability of the biosphere to absorb the effects of human activities.' (Chapter I.3.27).

In 2010, as the international community recommitted to accelerate efforts towards inclusive, sustainable development, the United Nations initiated a process towards defining a post-2015 global development agenda. The United Nations has sought a more inclusive approach than that which led to the Millennium Development Goals, and civil society has been particularly active in promoting this as well, with a particular aim to ensure that poorer countries are more involved in the design of goals and targets, and in developing the process for their implementation.

The process has engaged a number of parallel work streams to develop and refine what have come to be referred to as the Sustainable Development Goals, the most notable of which are the Intergovernmental Committee of Experts on Sustainable Development Financing, the High-Level Political Forum on Sustainable Development, the High-Level Panel of Eminent Persons on the Post-2015 Development Agenda, the Sustainable Development Solutions Network, the United Nations Open Working Group on Sustainable Development Goals, and a large number of in-country and thematic consultations.

The Intergovernmental Committee of Experts on Sustainable Development Financing grew out of the Rio+20 United Nations Conference on Sustainable Development. The Committee has worked closely with the United Nations Working Group on Financing for Sustainable Development to identify ways in which resources might be mobilised towards sustainable development.

The High-Level Political Forum on Sustainable Development is the main United Nations platform for post-2015 sustainable development, providing political leadership as well as coordinating the outputs of the various work streams. The Forum has worked closely with the various in-country, thematic, and regional consultations, including consultations on monitoring and accountability.

The High-Level Panel of Eminent Persons on the Post-2015 Development Agenda was launched in 2012 by the United Nations Secretary General. It was co-chaired by the Presidents of Indonesia and Liberia, and the Prime Minister of the UK. The Panel published its report in 2013, which called for five transformative shifts in the post-2015 agenda: fighting extreme poverty and inequality; putting sustainable development at the core of the post-2015 development agenda; transforming economies for jobs and inclusive growth; building peace and effective, open, and accountable institutions for all; and creating a new global partnership for development.

The Sustainable Development Solutions Network is an independent network of academic and non-academic researchers from around the world that supports the development of the Sustainable Development Goals. The Network published its report, *An Action Agenda for Sustainable Development*, in 2013. The report recommended 10 goals, which closely correspond thematically with the Open Working Group's proposal, presented below.

The United Nations Open Working Group on Sustainable Development Goals was established in 2013 by the General Assembly. It has become the primary mechanism for synthesising the processes mentioned above into a set of final goals. The Open Working Group held 13 meetings across 2013–14, the outcome of which was a proposal for 17 Sustainable Development Goals, and 169 indicators. These were finalised in the Report of the Open Working Group of the General Assembly on Sustainable Development Goals (Document A/68/970) in August 2014, before being presented to the United Nations General Assembly, New York in September 2014. The Open Working Group welcomed inputs from coalitions of interest groups, including civil society organisations and private sector interests. This process ensured that the goals reflected the views of a wide range of stakeholders; the international community welcomed the unprecedented inclusiveness and transparency of this process. The list of goals presented to the 2014 General Assembly is as follows:

Goal 1: End poverty in all its forms everywhere
Goal 2: End hunger, achieve food security and improved nutrition, and promote sustainable agriculture
Goal 3: Ensure healthy lives and promote wellbeing for all at all ages

Goal 4: Ensure inclusive and equitable quality education and promote lifelong learning opportunities for all

Goal 5: Achieve gender equality and empower all women and girls

Goal 6: Ensure availability and sustainable management of water and sanitation for all

Goal 7: Ensure access to affordable, reliable, sustainable, and modern energy for all

Goal 8: Promote sustained, inclusive, and sustainable economic growth, full and productive employment and decent work for all

Goal 9: Build resilient infrastructure, promote inclusive and sustainable industrialization, and foster innovation

Goal 10: Reduce inequality within and among countries

Goal 11: Make cities and human settlements inclusive, safe, resilient, and sustainable

Goal 12: Ensure sustainable consumption and production patterns

Goal 13: Take urgent action to combat climate change and its impacts[2]

Goal 14: Conserve and sustainably use the oceans, seas, and marine resources for sustainable development

Goal 15: Protect, restore, and promote sustainable use of terrestrial ecosystems, sustainably manage forests, combat desertification, and halt and reverse land degradation and halt biodiversity loss

Goal 16: Promote peaceful and inclusive societies for sustainable development, provide access to justice for all and build effective, accountable, and inclusive institutions at all levels

Goal 17: Strengthen the means of implementation and revitalize the global partnership for sustainable development

The resolution adopted on 14th September 2014 states that the Open Working Group's proposal will be the main basis for integrating the Sustainable Development Goals into the post-2015 agenda. After the General Assembly, countries began a 12-month process of in-country consultations and intergovernmental dialogues, in order to refine a final set of goals to be agreed and launched at the United Nations Summit to adopt the post-2015 development agenda in September 2015.

The 17 Sustainable Development Goals that have emerged from the Open Working Group discussions have clearly revealed the ways in which the new agenda will build upon and address some of the shortcomings of the Millennium Development Goals, as well as the limitations and challenges that remain; however, the vertical nature of many remains. While the new agenda is broader

---

[2] Acknowledging that the United Nations Framework Convention on Climate Change is the primary international, intergovernmental forum for negotiating the global response to climate change.

and more ambitious than the Millennium Development Goals, policy makers are not yet recognising the significance of how efforts to achieve one target will impact, positively or negatively, on efforts to achieve others.

Interactions will occur between the different sectors associated with these 17 goals whether we account for them or not. These interactions could be positive or negative, symmetrical or asymmetrical, physical, physiological, social or political. Some interactions, such as between health and education, or industrialisation and greenhouse gas emissions, are fairly well understood. But there are many other types of interaction, often with profound impacts on human welfare and well-being that are barely understood at all. How does the sustainable intensification of agriculture impact on climate change? How might efforts to reduce inequality within and between countries contribute to the development of sustainable, inclusive, cities and human settlements?

This book represents a collaborative research process that aims to examine and interrogate the current global development discourse, through concise academic commentary on sectoral debates, and by exploring the opportunities that might arise from understanding the complex interactions between development sectors, and the challenges for governance that this approach raises.

Part one of the book consists of concise commentaries on the current state of development debates in different sectors. Each chapter addresses the same set of questions:

- What is the historical process by which goal setting in this sector has developed?
- What progress has been achieved in this sector through the Millennium Development Goals and other processes?
- What is the current debate about future goal setting?

Part one concludes with a chapter on the governance of development goals, which we feel has particular importance to the design, implementation, and achievement of the Sustainable Development Goals over the next 15 years.

Part two of the book begins with a chapter that draws conclusions from our interdisciplinary efforts. It presents a novel conceptualisation of the 17 Sustainable Development Goals and their interactions, and uses this to show how potential synergies might be exploited and conflicts mitigated in their implementation. We conclude that effective governance of 'infrastructure' goals that directly link environmental sustainability to individual and collective wellbeing outcomes will be key to a post-2015 success. The second chapter comprises a case study that illustrates Sustainable Development Goal interactions, governance issues, and possible solutions around a particular cluster of goals on education, population, and health.

This book represents an effort to consider global development within and across sectors, and as a complex series of interactions. We hope that it will provoke discussion and engagement with the post-2015 development agenda, not only on how the goals themselves are developed, but also the far more important issues of how they might be governed, implemented and achieved to ensure sustainable, inclusive global development.

Contributors

As with any interdisciplinary process in academia, participants play many and diverse roles. Some make key contributions from their areas of expertise, others get involved in the process of generating understanding and consensus across these different areas, many do both. All are important and we acknowledge and thank all participants below. Contributors to specific outputs are cited as authors in the chapters which follow.

Editors

Jeff Waage. London International Development Centre; School of Oriental and African Studies, Centre for Development, Environment and Policy

Christopher Yap. London International Development Centre; University College London, Bartlett Development Planning Unit

Authors

Yoseph Araya. Birkbeck College, Department of Geography, Environment and Development Studies

Sarah Bell. University College London, Centre for Environmental and Geomatic Engineering

Tim Colbourn. University College London, Institute for Global Health

Ben Collen. University College London, Centre for Biodiversity and Environment Research

Anthony Costello. University College London, Institute for Global Health

Niheer Dasandi. University College London, School of Public Policy

Andrew Dorward. School of Oriental and African Studies, Centre for Environment, Development and Policy

Lucien Georgeson. University College London, Department of Geography

Jasmine Gideon. Birkbeck College, Department of Geography, Environment and Development Studies

Nora Groce. University College London, Leonard Cheshire Disability and Inclusive Development Centre

Michael Heinrich. University College London, School of Pharmacy

David Hudson. University College London, School of Public Policy

Ilan Kelman. University College London, Institute for Global Health and Institute for Risk and Disaster Reduction

Maria Kett. University College London, Leonard Cheshire Disability and Inclusive Development Centre

Richard Kock. Royal Veterinary College, Department of Pathology and Pathogen Biology

Sari Kovats. London School of Hygiene and Tropical Medicine, Department of Social and Environmental Research

Caren Levy. University College London, Bartlett Development Planning Unit

Georgina Mace. University College London, Centre for Biodiversity and Environment Research

Colin Marx. University College London, Bartlett Development Planning Unit

Mark Maslin. University College London, Department of Geography

Susannah H. Mayhew. London School of Hygiene and Tropical Medicine, Department of Global Health and Development

Andrew Newsham. School of Oriental and African Studies, Centre for Environment, Development and Policy

Tom Pegram. University College London, School of Public Policy

Nigel Poole. School of Oriental and African Studies, Centre for Environment, Development and Policy

Peter Sammonds. University College London, Department of Earth Sciences

David Satterthwaite. International Institute for Environment and Development; University College London, Bartlett Development Planning Unit

Laurence Smith. School of Oriental and African Studies, Centre for Development, Environment and Policy

Elaine Unterhalter. University College London Institute of Education, Department of Humanities and Social Sciences

Frauke Urban. School of Oriental and African Studies, Centre for Environment, Development and Policy

Paul Wilkinson. London School of Hygiene and Tropical Medicine, Department of Social and Environmental Health Research

Niall Winters. University of Oxford, Department of Education (previously affiliated to University College London Institute of Education)

Perspectives on the Post-2015 Sustainable Development Agenda

Biodiversity and ecosystems

Ben Collen[*], Richard Kock[†], Michael Heinrich[‡],
Laurence Smith[§] and Georgina Mace[*]

[*]University College London, Centre for Biodiversity and Environment Research, [†]Royal Veterinary College, Department of Pathology and Pathogen Biology, [‡]University College London, School of Pharmacy, [§]School of Oriental and African Studies, Centre for Environment, Development and Policy

What is the historical process by which goal setting in this sector has developed?

Biologists devised the word biodiversity to allow us to talk about the totality of life on Earth, encompassing everything from the level of DNA and genes, through to individuals, species, and whole ecosystems. Reducing global biodiversity loss in the face of unprecedented population extirpation and species extinction has become a fundamental goal for conservation, and the subject of an array of international, national, and regional policies and goals. The recognition that humans, in some way or other, rely on biodiversity and ecosystems for a great deal has bolstered and driven recent goal setting. The diversity of life we observe not only provides a rich and varied component of the natural world but, ironically, most is hidden in soils and seas and wantonly abused. Together, seen or unseen, they are our natural capital: the engineers and providers of the many benefits which humans accrue from an intact and fully functioning environment. In this chapter, we aim to summarise the developments in international goal setting and measurement for biodiversity and ecosystems; we focus on the past 25 years, when the majority of change has taken place.

How to cite this book chapter:
Collen, B, Kock, R, Heinrich, M, Smith, L, and Mace, G. 2015. Biodiversity and ecosystems. In: Waage, J and Yap, C. (eds.) *Thinking Beyond Sectors for Sustainable Development.* Pp. 3–9. London: Ubiquity Press. DOI: http://dx.doi.org/10.5334/bao.a

Prior to the international conventions of the 1990s, goal setting in this sector had largely been driven by a focus on specific species or a few selected habitats. There have subsequently been two strands of the development of goals and measures of biodiversity and ecosystem change emerging internationally (Mace et al. 2005). The first is the Convention on Biological Diversity (CBD), which was signed by a large number of participant nations in 1992 (the Rio Conventions). A range of programmes integrating strategies for improved human health and protection of global biodiversity have been developed from this convention. In addition, a wide range of other related conventions were created, including the United Nations Framework Convention on Climate Change (UNFCCC) and United Nations Convention to Combat Desertification (UNCCD). The CBD took a long time to develop any protocols for evaluating change in biodiversity and ecosystem, and setting goals to aim for, but set a target for biodiversity in 2010 (to slow the rate of loss; for examples see Balmford et al. 2005; Butchart et al. 2010; Mooney & Mace 2009; Walpole et al. 2010), followed by 20 targets for 2020, known as the Aichi Biodiversity Targets (an integrated set of targets across the goals of addressing causes, reducing pressures, enhancing benefits to people, and improving implementation through participatory planning).

The second strand was the Millennium Development Goals (MDGs), which independently developed a goal for environmental sustainability. Whether any progress was made towards achieving this goal was never seriously tested, though some indicators for measuring biodiversity were co-opted from the CBD process.

What progress has been achieved in this sector through the Millennium Development Goals and other processes?

On a broad scale, progress has been limited. In almost every way we measure biodiversity, decline is still apparent; pressures on biodiversity are growing in extent and intensity, and the few indicators that measure metrics that relate to human benefits from biodiversity are all in decline. More thought has gone into target setting though, and there is now a growing group of indicators to track progress (Butchart et al. 2004; Collen et al. 2009; Tittensor et al. 2014) aggregated population trends among vertebrate species indicate the rate of change in the status of biodiversity, and this index can be used to address the question of whether or not the 2010 target has been achieved. We investigated the use of generalized additive models in aggregating large quantities of population trend data, evaluated potential bias that results from collation of existing trends, and explored the feasibility of disaggregating the data (e.g., geographically, taxonomically, regionally, and by thematic area).

The progress that has been achieved has made been through the following mechanisms:

- Locally inspired and driven conservation efforts, usually species- or habitat-related, have successfully arrested local declines and species extinctions. The overall impact is negligible in relation to the extent of overall landscape change and biodiversity loss, but still highly significant and resilient. For example, black and white rhino conservation in Africa has had notable success in recovering and maintaining populations of these species. However, the vast majority are in fenced, ecologically unviable systems, and genetic exchange relies on a complex system of meta-population management, auction sales, and translocation, whilst the threat of poaching remains significant (Biggs et al. 2013).

- There are a large number of internationally inspired, funded, and driven projects to protect species and manage habitats or species, sometimes with local staffing, which show short-term positive results. The long-term sustainability of such progress is frequently threatened due to lack of local adoption or political turmoil. The saiga antelope is a case in point: after the collapse of the Soviet Union, a protection-focused management system disappeared almost overnight, and nearly one million animals were slaughtered for food and/or exploitation of commercially valued male horn, whilst agricultural and supply systems failed, leading to one of the most dramatic population crashes of a large mammal ever seen.

- Government driven and funded programmes have achieved notable success, particularly in areas of good governance and relatively high wealth. One example is the population recovery of large carnivores in the Rocky Mountain range of North America. There have also been many failures, especially in lower-middle income countries where insufficient resources are available to ensure conservation success. One leading problem is the lack of incentive for local human populations to conserve, in the face of protectionist policy and no local benefits to people. This is exemplified by the disappearance of species and populations from many of the so-called protected areas in South, South East and Central Asia; and East, Central and West Africa (Craigie et al. 2010).

What is the current debate about future goal setting?

Goal setting around the topic of biodiversity has generally been conducted in the context of preventive measures, and from the beginning these goals have often been in conflict with other global goals, for example those associated with agriculture and health. Most notably, agricultural and urban expansion are in constant conflict with goals to conserve biodiversity. Of note, these intersectorial conflicts have not been debated in any detail. There is a lot of interest in the CBD process, particularly from governments, policy makers, conservation organisations, and scientists, especially as some of the CBD goals are very much directed towards biodiversity conservation. Others have broad overlaps into commodity and production sectors, and into public education and health. A few questions that we believe need to be highlighted are:

- Are the 20 CBD targets all achievable simultaneously or do they conflict? The greatest gains will be made where there are mutual benefits among targets. For example, reducing habitat loss (Target 5) will be instrumental in allowing for the restoration of degraded ecosystems (Target 15) and reversing biodiversity trends (Target 12). There are also cases where target achievement appears to conflict with others, for example habitat restoration (e.g. Target 15) can come at the expense of habitat protection (Target 11) when resources allocated to conservation are limited.

- How should national and regional differences in responsibility for key biodiversity targets be addressed? For example the most threatened species are typically country endemic. For globally important ecosystems similar issues abound, such as tropical forests for carbon sequestration, open and deep ocean global commons, and the agricultural policies relating to land-sparing and land-sharing. Agriculture has by far the greatest negative influence on biodiversity and natural systems, with an estimated 38 per cent of global terrestrial land dedicated to this use. At current rates of conversion of land suited to agriculture, the areas of that agro-biotype to remain in a natural state will soon be negligible. Other impacts of, for example, water use for agriculture (currently at 95 per cent of available global freshwater supplies), will have considerable effect beyond these agro-ecological zones. The food security-agriculture-land use-aquaculture debate is largely ignored by the conservation community, which is focused on illegal killing, individual species conservation, and protectionist policies that are largely impotent in the face of agricultural development and other extractive industries.
- Are species the best indicators for biodiversity conservation? Species are considered by many to be the natural unit at which biodiversity change should be measured; however, perhaps a broader evaluation of the benefits from the land and sea that includes, but is not restricted to, species conservation might be more helpful for national decision-making (Bateman et al. 2013).
- Is 2020 the right time frame for multiple goals for biodiversity? Some of the metrics of biodiversity and ecosystems in which we are interested have very long and slow degradation and recovery times (e.g. coral reefs, tundra, and cod stocks), so it is not apparent whether targets are achievable within the time frames set. Moreover, natural population fluctuations require that datasets are sufficiently long to diagnose the difference between short-term dynamics and long-term trends.
- How should the CBD best interface with the UNFCCC and the Food and Agriculture Organization of the United Nations (FAO), which often deal with closely related issues, particularly if goals are conflicting?
- What is the role of monetary valuation and trade, and can the deleterious drivers of decline in biodiversity be turned to good effect? Examples of this are The Economics of Environment and Biodiversity (TEEB) initiative, the World Bank's Wealth Accounting and the Valuation of Ecosystem Services (WAVES) partnership, and natural capital accounting.

- Can the continuity of the indicator-goal-policy cycle be improved? The indicator-goal-policy cycle should ideally be iterative but there is a tendency to move from one set of goals to the next, with no real connexion between the two. Designing the goals and indicators coherently would streamline the process and increase the chances of achieving stated goals (Collen & Nicholson 2014).

Considerable attention has been paid to the use of the world's biodiversity for developing new high-value products (e.g. medicinal and engineering products), sustainable use of natural capital, and to the sharing of equitable benefits that stem from those products. Governance of the use of natural resources has historically been extremely weak, and only relatively recently have rights to biological property and their use been accepted at an international level, although they are rarely enforced. For example, the global agricultural industry based on the oil palm tree (the principal source of palm oil), an endemic of Guinea Conakry, accrued no benefits to its country of origin, which remains trapped in poverty, whilst global investors have continued to support and benefit from extractive industries.

Considerable attention has focused on developing new drug leads for use in globalised markets; primarily this is focused on more developed economies, the classical user-countries of such knowledge and materials. A good example of the benefits of mimicry of nature is the current research in Germany into novel antimicrobials, generated by insects (Hull et al. 2012; Steckbeck et al. 2014). This is critical research in the face of increasing antimicrobial resistance, now considered by the industrialised nations as the eighth most important threat to the economies of the world.

An aspect of biodiversity rarely accounted for is its buffering effect, along with ecosystem integrity, on emerging infectious diseases. This is a growing debate given the increasing rate of emergence of old and new infectious diseases. The hypothesis is based on the idea that development in, and fragmentation of forested systems in particular, may equate to a desterilising force allowing the spill-over of novel pathogens into amplifying host systems of domestic animals and people; the severe acute respiratory syndrome (SARS) virus, the Nipah virus, and the Ebola virus emergence are all examples of this potential. Finally, the value of harvesting systems, be it marine or terrestrial, remains high, and the capacity for renewal is remarkable despite global overexploitation. There exists no more sustainable system, but again the failure in governance of these resources, effectively considered a common good, has forced communities into increased reliance on agriculture and aquaculture. The net effect is global loss of biodiversity and habitat and less efficient production of food and goods. In general, it is a key goal of CBD targets to contribute to biodiversity conservation and economic development, both at an international and local level.

Biodiversity is traditionally associated with rural areas, but its importance in growing urban areas is increasingly recognised. Urban greening and urban biodiversity is an element of the Sustainable Development Goals (SDGs; the successors to the MDGs) that could help reconnect the vast majority of people to the concerns of biodiversity conservation, and provide real gains in health in urban environments. Maintenance of biodiversity underpins the achievement of many of the proposed SDGs, given its role in maintaining genetic diversity of food crops, supporting human health, providing future options for adaptation, and in providing supporting and provisioning services from ecosystems (Mace et al. 2014). There are several areas in which a consistent focus on biodiversity could be beneficial, but seriously tackling the social and economic context for future biodiversity conservation requires a shift in thinking and action for the whole of society.

References

Balmford, A., Bennun L. A., ten Brink B., Cooper D., Côté I. M., Crane P., Dobson D., et al. (2005). The Convention on Biological Diversity's 2010 target. *Science,* 307, 212–213. DOI: http://dx.doi.org/10.1126/science.1106281

Bateman, I. J., Harwood, A. R., Mace, G. M., Watson, R. T., Abson, D. J., Andrews, B., Binner, A., et al. (2013). Bringing ecosystem services into economic decision-making: land use in the United Kingdom. *Science,* 341(6141), 45–50. DOI: http://dx.doi.org/10.1126/science.1234379

Biggs, D., Courchamp, F., Martin, R., & Possingham, H. P. (2013). Legal Trade of Africa'S Rhino Horns. *Science,* 339(March), 1038–1039. DOI: http://dx.doi.org/10.1126/science.1229998

Butchart, S. H. M., Stattersfield, A. J., Bennun, L. A., Shutes, S. M., Resit Akça-kaya, H., Baillie, J. E. M., Stuart, S. N., et al. (2004). Measuring global trends in the status of biodiversity: red list indices for birds. *PLoS Biology,* 2(12), e383. DOI: http://dx.doi.org/10.1371/journal.pbio.0020383

Butchart, S. H. M., Walpole, M., Collen, B., van Strien, A., Scharleman, J. P. W., Almond, R. E. A., Baillie, J. E. M., et al. (2010). Global biodiversity: indicators of recent declines. *Science,* 328, 1164–1168. DOI: http://dx.doi.org/10.1126/science.1187512

Collen, B., Loh, J., Whitmee, S., McRae, L., Amin, R., & Baillie, J. E. M. (2009). Monitoring change in vertebrate abundance: the Living Planet Index. *Conservation Biology,* 23(2), 317–327. DOI: http://dx.doi.org/10.1111/j.1523-1739.2008.01117.x

Collen, B., & Nicholson, E. (2014). Taking the measure of change. *Science,* 166(October), 10–12. DOI: http://dx.doi.org/10.1126/science.1255772

Craigie, I. D., Baillie, J. E. M., Balmford, A., Carbone, C., Collen, B., Green, R. E., & Hutton, J. M. (2010). Large mammal population declines in Africa's protected areas. *Biological Conservation,* 143(9), 2221–2228. DOI: http://dx.doi.org/10.1016/j.biocon.2010.06.007

Hull, R., Katete, R., & Ntwasa, M. (2012). Therapeutic potential of antimicrobials peptides from insects. *Biotechnology and Molecular Biology Review*, 7(2), 31–47

Mace, G. M., Masundire, H., Baillie, J. E. M., Ricketts, T. H., Brooks, T. M., Hoffmann, M., Stuart, S. N., et al. (2005). Ecosystems and human well-being: current state and trends. Millennium Ecosystem Assessment. Washington: Island Press.

Mace, G. M., Reyers, B., Alkemade, R., Biggs, R., Chapin, F. S., Cornell, S. E., Díaz, S., et al. (2014). Approaches to defining a planetary boundary for biodiversity. *Global Environmental Change, 28*, 289–297. DOI: http://dx.doi.org/10.1016/j.gloenvcha.2014.07.009

Mooney, H., & Mace, G. (2009). Biodiversity policy challenges. *Science, 325*(5947), 1474. DOI: http://dx.doi.org/10.1126/science.1180935

Steckbeck, J. D., Deslouches, B., & Montelaro, R. C. (2014) Antimicrobial peptides: new drugs for bad bugs? *Expert Opinion on Biological Therapy.* DOI: http://dx.doi.org/10.1517/14712598.2013.844227

Tittensor, D. P., Walpole, M., Hill, S. L. L., Boyce, D. G., Britten, G. L., Burgess, N. D., Butchart, S. H. M., et al. (2014). A mid-term analysis of progress toward international biodiversity targets. *Science, 346*, 1–182. DOI: http://dx.doi.org/10.1126/science.1257484

Walpole, M., Almond, R. E. A., Besançon, C., Butchart, S. H. M., Carr, G. M., Collen, B., Collette, L., et al. (2010). Tracking progress toward the 2010 biodiversity target and beyond. *Sciene, 325*(5947), 1503–1504. DOI: http://dx.doi.org/10.1126/science.1175466

Climate and climate change

Ilan Kelman[*], Tim Colbourn[†], Anthony Costello[†],
Lucien Georgeson[‡], Sari Kovats[§], Mark Maslin[ˢ],
Andrew Newsham[**], Peter Sammonds[††],
Frauke Urban[**], Jeff Waage[‡‡] and Paul Wilkinson[§§]

[*]University College London, Institute for Global Health and Institute for Risk and Disaster Reduction, [†]University College London, Institute for Global Health, [‡]University College London, Department of Geography, [§]London School of Hygiene and Tropical Medicine, Department of Social and Environmental Research, [ˢ]University College London, Department of Geography, [**]School of Oriental and African Studies, Centre for Environment, Development and Policy, [††]University College London, Department of Earth Sciences, [‡‡]London International Development Centre; School of Oriental and African Studies, Centre for Development, Environment and Policy, [§§]London School of Hygiene and Tropical Medicine, Department of Social and Environmental Health Research

Introduction

In this chapter, we aim to summarise the developments in international goal setting for, and measurement of climate change. Two definitions are needed from the glossary of the Intergovernmental Panel on Climate Change (IPCC 2014):

Adaptation: The process of adjustment to actual or expected climate and its effects. In human systems, adaptation seeks to moderate harm or

---

How to cite this book chapter:
Kelman, I, Colbourn, T, Costello, A, Georgeson, L, Kovats, S, Maslin, M, Newsham, A, Sammonds, P, Urban, F, Waage, J, and Wilkinson P. 2015. Climate and climate change. In: Waage, J and Yap, C. (eds.) *Thinking Beyond Sectors for Sustainable Development.* Pp. 11–17. London: Ubiquity Press. DOI: http://dx.doi.org/10.5334/bao.b

exploit beneficial opportunities. In natural systems, human intervention may facilitate adjustment to expected climate and its effects.

Mitigation: A human intervention to reduce the sources or enhance the sinks of greenhouse gases.

Note that this definition of adaptation distinguishes between human and natural systems, which is not common practice in sustainability debates. The definition of mitigation is also different from that used in most other fields.

What is the historical process by which goal setting in this sector has developed?

Three examples of past processes are provided here: the international policy process, the international scientific process, and examples of non-international processes (for a more detailed discussion please see Maslin 2014).

The main international policy process on climate change is the UNFCCC Conference of the Parties (COP). It started by seeking an international legally binding treaty on goals for climate change mitigation, which led to the Kyoto Protocol, the only international legally binding treaty on the topic. The Kyoto Protocol includes the important principle of 'common but differentiated responsibilities', referring to 'Annex 1 countries' — namely the richer, more developed countries with historically the most emissions — as having more responsibility for climate change mitigation than other countries. The specific goal of the Kyoto Protocol was that the Annex 1 countries committed to reducing their overall emissions of such gases by at least five per cent below 1990 levels in the commitment period 2008 to 2012. Today, the UNFCCC COP process also covers aspects of climate change adaptation. The general consensus is that country governments have no real incentive to reduce their greenhouse gas emissions or even to help others to substantively adapt, so there will need to be major progress soon if a worthwhile agreement is to be achieved.

The main international scientific process is the Intergovernmental Panel on Climate Change (IPCC) that provides a statement on the synthesis and assessment of the current state of climate change science. Each IPCC report undergoes a government review process and the *Summary for Policymakers* is debated and agreed by the member governments, currently numbering 195; thus, the report represents a political consensus of the current state of scientific knowledge. In the IPCC report from 2013–2014, the *Fifth Assessment Report* (*AR5*), new future greenhouse gas emissions scenarios called Representative Concentration Pathways (RCPs) are used. Relative to earlier scenarios, they consider a much wider variable input to the social-economic models including population, land use, energy intensity, energy use, and regionally differentiated development. These RCPs have been constructed to illustrate the consequences of different regional and global political policies up until 2100.

Other processes have developed their own goals outside of the UNFCCC and IPCC processes, such as:

- In 2008, the United Nations Environment Programme (UNEP) started a Climate Neutral Network with countries such as Costa Rica, cities such as Arendal in Norway, and corporations such as Senoko Energy Pte Ltd (a Singaporean power company), aiming for clear carbon-related targets. The Network closed in 2011.
- The World Business Council for Sustainable Development adopted the goal of limiting global temperature rise to 2°C above pre-industrial levels under their Action2020 plan, launched in 2013. Many member companies are now collaborating and developing sustainable investment mechanisms.
- The UK government passed the 2008 Climate Change Act, which established the world's first legally binding climate change target. The UK aims to reduce its greenhouse gas emissions by at least 80 per cent (from the 1990 baseline) by 2050.
- Binding EU legislation (The 2020 climate and energy package), known as the 20-20-20 targets, set three key objectives for 2020:
  - A 20 per cent reduction in EU greenhouse gas emissions from 1990 levels;
  - Raising the share of EU energy consumption produced from renewable resources to 20 per cent;
  - A 20 per cent improvement in the EU's energy efficiency.
- Mexico became the world's second country to pass legally binding targets, including a 30 per cent reduction in the growth of greenhouse gas emissions by 2020 and 50 per cent by 2050.
- The Carbon Disclosure Project (CDP) monitors emissions from companies and 120 cities.
- Since 2008 the *Harvard University Sustainability Plan*, which is developed by a task force of students, academics, and staff, has set goals for emissions and energy as well as promoting the use of research to increase efficiency on campus.
- Pension funds and shareholder action has led to divestment campaigns against fossil fuel companies. As one example, the Universities Superannuation Scheme (USS) pension scheme in the U.K. has a campaign regarding ethical investment http://listentouss.org while a report by Cleveland and Reibstein (2015) describes opportunities for universities to divest from fossil fuels.
- The Sustainable Energy for All (SE4A) initiative has three objectives to be achieved by 2030, one of which is achieving universal access to modern energy services. The International Energy Agency estimates that this will partly be achieved by small-scale, decentralised, renewable energy technology that will contribute to climate change mitigation.

At times, the wider green agenda (including biodiversity conservation, pollution prevention, and tackling environmental contamination) has been seen as synonymous with the climate change mitigation agenda. In reality, climate change mitigation efforts can cause or exacerbate environmental problems, with literature showing how carbon capture and storage/sequestration (CCS), carbon offsets, large-scale geoengineering, and the United Nations Collaborative Programme on Reducing Emissions from Deforestation and Forest Degradation (UN-REDD) programme are neither particularly environmentally friendly nor effective for tackling climate change (Beymer-Farris & Bassett 2012; Dodds et al. 2012). Instead, climate change mitigation should be viewed as necessary, but not sufficient for an overall green agenda, and wider contexts should always be considered.

What progress has been achieved in this sector through the Millennium Development Goals and other processes?

Historically, the climate change agenda focused on mitigation. When adaptation was first discussed, many adamantly opposed a shift in focus because they felt that it was giving up the fight to stop climate change and adopting a fatalistic view; implying that we must deal with climate change because we cannot stop it. Now, both mitigation and adaptation are accepted as necessary. In fact, when the IPCC and UNFCCC COP processes were starting, many advocated for joining mitigation and adaptation. Instead, the two processes were explicitly separated, which continued despite literature showing their complementarity (Dang, Michaelowa & Tuan 2003; Kane & Shogren 2000). Finally, some movement is now being made at the IPCC and UNFCCC COP levels to show how mitigation and adaptation can, and should, support each other and are not separate activities.

Some programmes with various degrees of success (many are voluntary with no real enforcement mechanism and often without adequate monitoring mechanisms) are:

- The UNFCCC COP process led to the Kyoto Protocol, with its legally binding mitigation target, which was not fully reached.
- The IPCC continues to publish a periodic synthesis and assessment of the political consensus of the current state of scientific knowledge on climate change science, while delving into more specific topics through special reports on, for example, renewable energy sources and extreme events. The IPCC has also made progress on capacity for metrics and measurements, but there are nonetheless problems with establishing emissions baselines due to uptake of greenhouse gases by the oceans and the biosphere.
- The UK, EU, and Mexico climate change targets are currently legally binding, but they could nonetheless be rescinded later.
- The UN-REDD and related processes have encountered problems as sequestration due to reforestation and other activities is not well-documented or easily documentable.

- Under the UNFCCC, the United Nations-designated Least Developed Countries (LDCs) are mandated to produce national adaptation programmes of action (NAPAs) to summarise and build on existing strategies and knowledge. Also under the UNFCCC, developing countries can report nationally appropriate mitigation actions (NAMAs).
- The Clean Development Mechanism (CDM) under the Kyoto Protocol permits developed countries to gain carbon credits for implementing emission-reduction projects in developing countries. The CDM is considered to have failed because it operates only at the international level, whereas multilevel governance and multiple mechanisms are needed and must be connected. Otherwise, abuse of CDM approaches, deliberate or inadvertent, can occur, as shown in Latin America (Lokey 2009).
- Regional Climate Innovation Centres have been set up in several developing countries, including Kenya and the Caribbean, with the aim of increasing research and development, testing, and diffusion of climate-relevant innovation, for both mitigation and adaptation.

What is the current debate about future goal setting?

There are three principal approaches to mitigation:

- The current political consensus is to limit the average global mean temperature rise to 2°C. Although this is not enshrined in any international agreement, it is repeatedly referenced by the UNFCCC, the EU, and the Small Island Developing States (SIDS). The global mean temperature record has been instrumental in focusing attention on climate change, and is a simple and clear metric for politicians to use for assessing progress and failure. It does not capture the full range of climate change impacts or the problem of potentially irreversible changes. The carbon budget to keep temperature rises below 2°C is likely to be spent by 2040.
- Another approach is to be under a specific average global level of parts per million (ppm) of CO_2 (equivalent) in the atmosphere. Note that a specific temperature rise does not give a unique ppm solution (and vice versa), which creates a political problem, because an outcome is not clear for a given target. Examples of ppm levels suggested are 350 ppm (Hansen et al. 2008) and 300 ppm (Target 300 Campaign 2015). At the global scale, the atmospheric concentration of CO_2 has increased from a preindustrial value of approximately 280 ppm to above 400 ppm (Tans & Keeling 2013).
- A third example of an approach is to seek alternatives to globally averaged quantitative targets. One example is two tonnes per person per year of carbon, as advocated by the Global Commons Institute since 1989, which could also suggest personal goals for CO_2 or CO_2 equivalents. If the

individual limit is then slowly reduced, this yields a form of the Contraction and Convergence approach.

A significant impediment to future goal setting is that the UNFCCC COP and IPCC processes are consensual rather than democratic, leading to significant trouble in getting all parties on board all the time. That has meant that the trajectory of emission reduction is seen as proceeding far too slowly, with many emissions left out of control regimes, such as international shipping and aviation. The EU wanted to include aviation in the already existing EU Emissions Trading System, but an uproar followed and the plan was not fulfilled. Similarly, Australia passed a carbon tax in 2012, which was later rescinded following a change in government two years later.

For adaptation, the main targets relate to reducing any losses and damage from climate change impact, which has long been part of disaster risk reduction and development targets, such as the *Hyogo Framework for Action* and the MDGs/SDGs (Kelman & Gaillard 2010). For mitigation and adaptation goals, many debates have long examined how to better integrate climate change with other development-related endeavours, as well as the long-standing efforts to stop the separation between mitigation and adaptation mentioned above. Furthermore, attribution of climate hazards to climate change is problematic, while 'adaptive capacity' can indicate the ability to deal with any development-related phenomena, whether linked to climate change or not.

References

Beymer-Farris, B. A., & Bassett, T. J. (2012). The REDD menace: resurgent protectionism in Tanzania's mangrove forests. *Global Environmental Change*, 22(2), 332–341. DOI: http://dx.doi.org/10.1016/j.gloenvcha.2011.11.006

Cleveland, C. J., & R. Reibstein (2015). The Path to Fossil Fuel Divestment for Universities: Climate Responsible Investment. Department of Earth and Environment, Boston University. Retrieved from http://energyincontext.com/wp-content/uploads/2015/02/University-Divestment-Fossil-Fuels-Cleveland_Reibstein_02_13_15.pdf

Dang, H. H., Michaelowa, A., & Tuan, D. D. (2003). Synergy of adaptation and mitigation strategies in the context of sustainable development: the case of Vietnam. *Climate Policy*, 3S1, S81–S96. DOI: http://dx.doi.org/10.1016/j.clipol.2003.10.006

Dodds, R., Kelman, I., Thiesen, N., McDougall, A., Garcia, J. & Bessada, T. (2012). Industry Perspectives on Carbon Offsetting Programs in Canada and the USA. *Sustainability: Science, Practice, & Policy*, 8(2), 31–41.

European Commission (EC). (Last updated 30 April 2015). *The 2020 climate and energy package.* Retrieved from http://ec.europa.eu/clima/policies/package/index_en.htm

Hansen, J., Sato, M., Kharecha, P., Beerling, D., Berner, R., Masson-Delmotte, V., Pagani, M., Raymo, M., Royer, D.L. & Zachos, J.C. (2008). Target atmospheric CO2: Where should humanity aim? *Open Atmospheric Science Journal*, *2*, 217–231, DOI: http://dx.doi.org/10.2174/1874282300802010217

Intergovernmental Panel on Climate Change (IPCC). (2014). *IPCC Fifth Assessment Report: Working Group II*. (AR5: 31st Session of the IPCC in Bali, 26–29 October 2009). IPCC, Geneva, Switzerland.

Kane, S., & Shogren, J. F. (2000). Linking Adaptation and Mitigation in Climate Change Policy. *Climatic Change*, *45*, 75–102. DOI: http://dx.doi.org/10.1023/A:1005688900676

Kelman, I., & Gaillard, J. C. (2010). Embedding climate change adaptation within disaster risk reduction. In R. Shaw, J. M. Pulhin, & J. J. Pereira (Eds.), *Climate change adaptation and disaster risk reduction: issues and challenge*. 23–46. Bingley: Emerald Group Publishing Limited. DOI: http://dx.doi.org/10.1108/S2040-7262(2010)0000004008

Lokey, E. (2009). Renewable energy project development under the clean development mechanism: a guide for Latin America. London: Earthscan Publishers.

Maslin, M. (2014). Climate change: a very short introduction, 3rd ed. Oxford: Oxford University Press.

Tans, P., & Keeling, R. (2013). Trends in atmospheric carbon dioxide. NOAA/ESRL, Boulder, Colorado and Scripps Institution of Oceanography, San Diego, California. Retrieved from http://www.esrl.noaa.gov/gmd/ccgg/trends

Target 300 Campaign (2015). http://www.target300.org accessed on 8 May 2015.

Urbanisation and urban poverty reduction in low- and middle-income countries

Caren Levy[*], Colin Marx[*] and David Satterthwaite[†]

[*]University College London, Bartlett Development Planning Unit, [†]International Institute for Environment and Development; University College London, Bartlett Development Planning Unit

What is the historical process by which goal setting in this sector has developed?

Goal setting has a longer history in international development than is recognised, and we explore this before addressing contemporary concerns on urban poverty.

All official international development assistance is justified by its apparent contribution to reducing poverty, both urban and rural. But during the 1960s, the focus was on economic growth and its underpinnings, such as an educated labour force and economic infrastructure. There was an important new discourse from the late 1960s on the need for development assistance to address social issues, including poverty. The recommendation that more attention be paid to social issues as an end in itself can be seen in the report of a United Nations expert group meeting held in 1969 (United Nations 1971). A critique of conventional aid policies and the demand for more attention to the needs of poorer groups is also evident in the work of Myrdal (1968, 1970). The Pearson Commission, set up to review the successes and failures of aid, included in its recommendations a greater emphasis on 'social' projects, although this was not one of its central concerns (Mason & Asher 1973).

How to cite this book chapter:
Levy, C, Marx, C, and Satterthwaite D. 2015. Urbanisation and urban poverty reduction in low- and middle-income countries. In: Waage, J and Yap, C. (eds.) *Thinking Beyond Sectors for Sustainable Development.* Pp. 19–27. London: Ubiquity Press. DOI: http://dx.doi.org/10.5334/bao.c

The World Bank was among the first of the official development assistance agencies to make explicit its support for a higher priority to 'basic needs' and for targets to monitor this. For instance, in a speech in 1972, the Bank's President Robert McNamara called for nations

> 'to give greater priority to establishing growth targets in terms of essential human needs: in terms of nutrition, housing, health, literacy and employment - even if it be at the cost of some reduction in the pace of advance in certain narrow and highly privileged sectors whose benefits accrue to the few' (Clark 1981: 173).

An analysis of World Bank lending priorities shows a clear increase in the late 1970s to the priority given to meeting basic needs (Satterthwaite 1997 & 2001). Various books have recommended a greater priority to basic needs, including ul Haq (1976), Ward and Dubos (1972), and Ward (1976). Indeed, in Ward's *The Home of Man* (1976) there is a chapter entitled *The cost of justice* that draws on World Bank estimates for the investments needed over one decade for meeting needs for food and nutrition, education, rural and urban water supply, urban housing, urban transport, population, and health.

Between 1972 and 1978, many development assistance agencies and multilateral banks made explicit their support for increased allocations to basic needs; although with differing views as to what constituted basic needs (see for instance, ILO 1976; Sandbrook 1982; Streeten et al. 1981; Wisner 1988; Wood 1986), and the extent to which it was compatible with economic growth (e.g. 'redistribution with growth').

The global conferences organised by the United Nations on key problems that began with the Conference on the Human Environment in Stockholm in 1972 also began to make recommendations with all government representatives to these Conferences, formally endorsing them, and these included many goals, with a few including targets. For instance, in the United Nations Conference on Human Settlements in Vancouver in 1976, the *Vancouver Action Plan Recommendations for National Action* (United Nations 1976) endorsed by all attending government representatives included the following:

> 'Safe water supply and hygienic waste disposal should receive priority with a view to achieving measurable qualitative and quantitative targets serving all the population by a certain date: targets should be established by all nations and should be considered by the forthcoming United Nations Conference on Water. [...] In most countries urgent action is necessary to adopt programmes with realistic standards for quality and quantity to provide water for urban and rural areas by 1990, if possible' (United Nations 1976: Recommendation C.12).

There are links here with some of the books noted above, since Ward and Dubos' book (1972), entitled *Only One Earth: The Care and Maintenance of a*

Small Planet, was commissioned by the United Nations as a book for a general audience on the issues being discussed at the 1972 Conference on the Human Environment. Furthermore, Ward's work (1976) was commissioned by the Canadian Government who were hosting the 1976 United Nations Conference on Human Settlements. Barbara Ward also toured Canada just before the Conference, and organised a meeting of experts that promoted clear goals and targets on water and sanitation, and urged government delegates to the Conference to set and approve these.

During the 1970s, there is also evidence of some official development assistance agencies giving more attention to urban poverty. The World Bank began supporting 'slum/squatter upgrading' programmes and site and service schemes (for example, in Nairobi, Kenya; Amman, Jordan; and Cairo, Egypt), and during the 1970s, increased its support of initiatives to reduce urban poverty (Satterthwaite 1997).

Another important goal and target was set at the International Conference on Primary Health Care in Almaty (previously Alma-Ata) in 1978.

> 'A main social target of governments, international organisations and the whole world community in the coming decades should be the attainment by all peoples of the world by the year 2000 of a level of health that will permit them to lead a socially and economically productive life. Primary health care is the key to attaining this target as part of development in the spirit of social justice.' (WHO & UNICEF, 1978: 1)

These commitments to addressing basic needs and to universal provision (for water, sanitation, and primary health care) tended to disappear as priority issues in the 1980s, in part because of the global recession (what is termed 'the lost decade' in Latin America), and in part because of the change in the orientation of most development assistance agencies, associated with economic policies of Thatcher and Reagan. There was also a shift in some agencies and professionals to 'selective primary health care', that sought to prioritise what were judged to be the most cost-effective interventions, but that were also cheaper and easier to implement and still left key needs unmet, including provision for water and sanitation. The commitments to meeting needs re-emerged in the 1990s, in part within discussions of human development,[3] and then within the Organisation for Economic Co-operation and Development's (OECD's) International Development Targets in 1995 (whose purpose was to get more popular support for aid agencies in high-income countries) that then led to the United Nation's MDGs in 2000.

---

[3] Although many of the proponents of human development sought to distance themselves from the proponents of basic needs, there is considerable common ground between the two.

Thus, the MDGs in relation to urbanisation and urban poverty reduction are built on a long tradition of goal setting and international agreements in relation to broader developmental concerns. The MDGs' target of halving, between 1990 and 2015, the proportion of people whose income is less than US$1.25 per day, addresses the goal of eradicating extreme poverty within a broader goal that addresses poverty and hunger as interrelated. The MDGs contain one explicit urban target in relation to what are termed 'slums': to achieve, by 2020, a significant improvement in the lives of at least 100 million slum dwellers. This is a rather odd target as it is much less ambitious than other quantitative targets (it is seeking to cut the number of people living in slums by 10 per cent, and not to halve or reduce by two thirds as in other MDGs) and it is for 2020, not 2015. It also sits a little uncomfortably within a goal on ensuring environmental sustainability.

What progress has been achieved in this sector through the Millennium Development Goals and other processes?

It is difficult to assess progress in urban areas because of the (often very large) undercount in official statistics for those living in poverty, and because of inaccurate or inappropriate measures. The work of the World Health Organization (WHO) and the World Bank on disease and injury burdens, and on disability-adjusted life years (DALYs), provides a stronger basis for determining the most cost-effective interventions, but these are mostly done at national levels and so miss the (often large) differences in the ranking of disease and injury burdens between different locations within nations. They also do not provide the data needed by local governments, for instance the disease and injury burdens by ward or district.

The United Nations claims great progress towards most of the MDGs. In a report published in September 2013, the Secretary-General of the United Nations, Ban Ki-moon, said the MDGs 'have been the most successful global anti-poverty push in history' (UN 2013: 3). He added,

> 'Significant and substantial progress has been made in meeting many of the targets — including halving the number of people living in extreme poverty and the proportion of people without sustainable access to improved sources of drinking water. The proportion of urban slum dwellers declined significantly' (UN, 2013: 3).

However, much of the supporting evidence for these claims is based on faulty statistics or heroic guesses where there is no data. In regard to extreme poverty, the 2013 MDGs Report states that 'the proportion of people living in extreme poverty has been halved at the global level' (UN, Ibid: 4). But this is only because the United Nations uses an unrealistic poverty line of US$1.25 a day. In most cities, this is not enough to pay for food and non-food needs (Mitlin &

Satterthwaite 2012). If accurate poverty lines were set in each nation based on what food and non-food needs actually costs, the proportion of people in extreme poverty would have declined far less than the United Nations claims.

Set a poverty line low enough and much of the poverty will disappear. In applying the US$1.25 poverty line, there appears to be virtually no urban poverty in China, the Middle East, North Africa, and Central Asia, and very little in Latin America. Why then, are hundreds of millions of urban dwellers in these regions — who apparently are not poor — still living in poverty in poor quality, overcrowded homes that lack safe and sufficient water, sanitation, drainage, health care, and emergency services? Why are so many of their children malnourished? It is not difficult to conclude that their poverty is not 'extreme' enough for the United Nations to include them in their statistics.

In regard to provision of water, the 2013 MDGs Report states that 'over two billion people gained access to improved sources of drinking water' between 1990 and 2010, and 60 per cent of these were in urban areas; but this was only because the bar is set so low. Under United Nations definitions, a household has improved provision for water even if it only has access to a public tap or standpipe; so someone is said to have improved water even if they share a public tap with hundreds of others. The United Nations definition of improved water says nothing about whether it is available, affordable, or even potable.

The 2013 MDGs Report states that 'the proportion of slum dwellers in the cities and metropolises of the developing world is declining' (UN 2013: 4). It also states that 'many countries across all regions have shown remarkable progress in reducing the proportion of urban slum dwellers' (Ibid: 4), and that between 2000 and 2010, conditions improved for more than 200 million people so they were no longer living in slums. It even added that 'between 2010 and 2012 alone, conditions improved to the point where an additional 44 million people were no longer considered to be living in slums' (Ibid: 50).

Claims have been made by the United Nations that the proportion of India's urban population living in slums fell from 42 to 29 per cent between 2000 and 2010, and that there have been very significant falls in the proportion of urban populations living in slums in Bangladesh, Uganda, Angola, and the Democratic Republic of the Congo (Mitlin and Satterthwaite 2012). However, the supporting evidence for this can be questioned. It is very difficult for UN-Habitat, the institution that produces these slum statistics, to show changes in slum populations by year. Censuses can reveal detailed data about slums but they take place only every 10 years and many low-income nations have had no census in recent years. Household surveys that may provide limited data on slums are also not undertaken each year.

In regard to sanitation, the 2013 MDGs Report states 'gains in sanitation are impressive — but not good enough'. But here too, the bar is set so low that what is measured has no relation to what people need in urban contexts: a toilet in their home with good provision for disposing of excreta and for washing. A household is said to have improved sanitation even if it only has a pit latrine with a slab.

The 2013 MDGs Report, like so many United Nations documents, repeats a common view that conditions are worse in rural areas. But in large part, this is because it is inappropriate to set the same indicators for rural and urban areas. The definition for improved water and sanitation is the same for both rural and urban areas, despite the different contexts. So is the US$1.25 a day poverty line, suggesting that food and non-food costs are the same in rural areas and large cities. In most urban areas, much of the low-income population must pay a substantial proportion of their income for housing, water, and to use toilets. They often have to pay for (very poor quality) schools and health care because, as 'illegal settlers', they do not quality for publicly funded social services (Mitlin & Satterthwaite 2012).

A constant theme running through this chapter is how the local government institutions with responsibility for addressing different aspects of poverty are not engaged in making relevant commitments. There is the same disjuncture in regard to data: the MDGs rely mostly on national sample surveys to measure and monitor progress, including the Demographic and Health Surveys Program. But their sample sizes are too small to provide data on the geographic distribution of different deprivations. Local governments need data that can produce maps of exactly where those lacking provision for piped water, sanitation, and health care live at the level of their street or ward. Censuses can provide this, but national census authorities often refuse to provide the detailed data to local governments to allow this, and of course censuses usually only take place once every 10 years, if that. If it falls to local governments to implement many of the MDGs and many of the new set of goals and targets of the post-2015 process, then the collection and availability of data should be serving their needs.

Thus, while most of the responsibility for providing basic services and addressing other aspects of deprivation in urban areas fall to local governments, they often have new mandates, goals, and targets put upon them by national governments without the funds and support needed to act[4]. In most countries, these are also held to account for their performance in doing so in local elections and it is with this level of government that most citizens with unmet needs or facing deprivations actually interact.

In summary, it is difficult if not impossible to measure progress made to urban poverty in the past 10 years, but beyond the difficulties in measurement, there must surely be recognisable trends and change within the MDGs lifespan. Looking across the goals, it seems that progress made towards water goals, however limited or flawed, significantly outstripped progress made towards for example, improving maternal health.

---

[4] Similar problems arise in three other key urban agendas that need to be addressed – disaster risk reduction, climate change adaptation/resilience and climate change mitigation. National governments make commitments but much of what needs to change depends on local governments.

What is current debate about future goal setting?

The debate at the moment for the Post-2015 SDGs is on:

- whether these goals should have a stand-alone urban goal with its own set of targets and indicators;
- whether goals should be universal and with the same targets and indicators for rural and urban areas;
- or whether goals should be a modification of the latter, i.e., universal but with different targets and indicators used for rural and urban areas;
- how to incorporate cross-cutting issues such as gender.

These options are set in the context of an increasing urban challenge, with approximately 50 per cent of the world's population living in urban areas in 2008, and this figure is estimated to rise to 75 per cent in 2050. Since September 2013, a global Urban SDG Campaign was launched, made up of many institutions (including United Cities and Local Governments who represent local governments within the United Nations system) to lobby for a stand-alone urban goal. As illustrated above, the challenges of developing a stand-alone urban goal are many. Urban contexts have a set of characteristics that is distinct from rural contexts, and it is important for targets and indicators to recognise this difference. Of course, this is complicated by the great diversity in rural and urban contexts: what might be considered as urban contexts (high density, lack of open space, high levels of overcrowding, difficulty finding land on which to grow food and/or raise livestock, large distances between home and workplace, and access to highly monetised housing) are not present in all urban contexts, and are present in some rural contexts. These complex differences throw doubt on the validity of targets and their measurement to set the same monetary poverty line for rural and urban areas if many urban residents face much higher costs; and the same doubt applies to using the same indicators for access to water and sanitation, as well as many others.

In addition, the urban context is an increasingly important arena in which to address questions of justice, not only in terms of class but also by gender, age, ethnicity, race, religion and disability. Inequalities in cities have strong gender and other social identity dimensions (Levy, 2002; UN Habitat, 2012; Levy, 2013). The challenge is how to reflect and address these unequal cross cutting intersectional identities in the post-2015 goals, targets and indicators.

As of June 2014, the UN Open Working Group on Sustainable Development Goals proposed 17 goals, including a stand-alone urban goal, Goal 11, which focuses on 'making cities and human settlements inclusive, safe, resilient, and sustainable' (UN Open Working Group, 2014). This goal proposes 7 targets to be met by 2030, ranging from access for all to adequate, safe and affordable housing and basic services, energy efficient transport, efficient land use through participatory management, promotion of cultural and natural heritage, reduction of risk and disaster impacts, reduce environmental impacts of cities, and access to safe, inclusive and multi-purpose public space (Ibid). The proposed indicators for these targets are disaggregated by income, gender, age and disability, where appropriate. (UN Urban SDG Campaign, 2015: 5-13). An important concern for the Urban SDG Campaign is that 'the productive role of cities in adding economic value and creating informal and formal livelihoods' is not recognised in Goal 11, not least because it will 'provide the basis for the implementation and financing of key SDGs' (Ibid: 4). The forthcoming intergovernmental negotiations will be decisive in the future shape of Goal 11, which reflects the greater interest within development discussion in the role of cities and their governments in meeting many of the sustainable development goals.

References

Clark, W. (1981). Robert McNamara at the World Bank. *Foreign Affairs, Fall*, 167–184.

International Labour Office (ILO). (1976). *Basic needs and national employment strategies; background papers vol 1*. Paper presented at the Tripartite World Conference on Employment, Income Distribution and Social Progress and the International Division of Labour, International Labour Office, Geneva, Switzerland.

Levy, C. (2002). Towards the just city: gender and planning. In M. Balbo (Ed), *The inclusive city: issues for the city of developing countries*. Milano: Franco Angeli (in Italian and Spanish).

Levy, C. (2013). "Travel Choice Reframed: 'Deep Distribution' and Gender in Urban Transport", *Environment and Urbanization*, Vol. 25(1), 47–63

Mason, E. S., & Asher, R. (1973). The World Bank since Bretton Woods. Washington DC: The Brookings Institution.

Mitlin, D., & Satterthwaite, D. (2012). Urban poverty in the global south: scale and nature. London: Routledge.

Myrdal, G. (1968). Asian drama: an inquiry into the poverty of nations. London: Allan Lane/The Penguin Press.

Myrdal, G. (1970). The challenge of world poverty. London: Allan Lane/The Penguin Press.

Sandbrook, R. (1982). The politics of basic needs: urban aspects of assaulting poverty in Africa. London: Heinemann Educational.

Satterthwaite, D. (1997). The scale and nature of international donor assistance to housing, basic services and other human settlements-related projects. Helsinki: WIDER.

Satterthwaite, D. (2001). Reducing urban poverty: constraints on the effectiveness of aid agencies and development banks and some suggestions for change. *Environment and Urbanisation, 13*(1), 137–157.

Streeten, P. (1981). First things first - meeting basic needs in developing countries. Oxford: Oxford University Press.

ul Haq, M. (1976). The poverty curtain; choices for the Third World. New York: Columbia University Press.

United Nations. (1971). "Report of the 1969 meeting of exports on social policy and planning", International Social Development Review, No. 3.

United Nations. (1976). *United Nations Conference on Human Settlements: The Vancouver Action Plan*. Retrieved from http://www.un-documents.net/van-plan.htm

United Nations (2013). The Millennium Development Goals Report 2013. New York: United Nations.

United Nations Open Working Group (2014) Introduction to the Proposal of The Open Working Group for Sustainable Development Goals, Issued 19 July. Retrieved from https://sustainabledevelopment.un.org/focussdgs.html

UN Urban SDG Campaign, Second Urban Sustainable Development Goal Campaign Consultation on Targets and Indicators: Bangalore Outcome Document, Indian Institute for Human Settlements (IIHS) Bangalore City campus 12-14th January 2015. Retrieved from http://urbansdg.org/wp-content/uploads/2015/02/Urban_SDG_Campaign_Bangalore_Outcome_Document_2015.pdf

Ward, B. (1976). The Home of Man. New York: W.W. Norton & Company.

Ward, B., & Dubos, R. (1972). *Only* one earth: the care and maintenance of a small planet. London: Andre Deutsch.

Wisner, B. (1988). Power and need in Africa: basic human needs and development policies. London: Earthscan Publications.

Wood, R. E. (1986). From Marshall Plan to debt crisis: foreign aid and development choices in the world economy. Berkley: University of California Press.

World Health Organisation and UNICEF. (1978) Declaration of Alma-Ata, International Conference on Primary Health Care, Alma-Ata, USSR, 6–12 September 1978, Section V. Retrieved from http://www.who.int/publications/almaata_declaration_en.pdf

Human health

Tim Colbourn[*], Jasmine Gideon[†], Nora Groce[‡],
Michael Heinrich[§], Ilan Kelman[ʿ], Maria Kett[‡],
Richard Kock[**], Susannah H. Mayhew[††]
and Jeff Waage[‡‡]

[*]University College London, Institute for Global Health, [†]Birkbeck College, Department of Geography, Environment and Development Studies, [‡]University College London, Leonard Cheshire Disability and Inclusive Development Centre, [§]University College London, School of Pharmacy, [ʿ]University College London, Institute for Global Health and Institute for Risk and Disaster Reduction, [**]Royal Veterinary College, Department of Pathology and Pathogen Biology, [††]London School of Hygiene and Tropical Medicine, Department of Global Health and Development, [‡‡]London International Development Centre; School of Oriental and African Studies, Centre for Development, Environment and Policy

What is the historical process by which goal setting in this sector has developed?

In high-income countries, goal setting in the sphere of human health has had a national focus, with governments setting targets in response to lobbying from a combination of interest groups. These groups include bodies of health professionals and experts, non-governmental organisations (NGOs) and charities, and industry and media, and public pressure has been exerted via the influence of all of these groups. Middle-income countries that have a degree of representative democracy have followed similar processes, and are therefore becoming less connected or bound to global development agendas, including those on human health. These countries are instead becoming more

How to cite this book chapter:
Colbourn, T, Gideon, J, Groce, N, Heinrich, M, Kelman, I, Kett, M, Kock, R, Mayhew, S. H., and Waage, J. 2015. Human health. In: Waage, J and Yap, C. (eds.) *Thinking Beyond Sectors for Sustainable Development.* Pp. 29–36. London: Ubiquity Press. DOI: http://dx.doi.org/10.5334/bao.d

focused on their own development plans, developed from within their borders or through regional bodies and economic groupings.

In contrast, goal setting in human health in low-income countries has, and continues to be, predominantly influenced by international organisations such as the WHO, UNICEF, and the United Nations Population Fund (UNFPA), and donor institutions upon which many low-income countries remain dependent. The last 15 years or so have seen a shift towards the influence of private philanthropic donor institutions such as the Bill & Melinda Gates Foundation (BMGF), but high-income-country government donors such as the United States Agency for International Development (USAID) and the UK Department for International Development (DFID) remain very influential, since they are major sources of funding for many low-income countries, especially in relation to human health. These donors, along with other interested parties from high-income countries, also fund global initiatives, such as the Global Fund to Fight AIDS, Tuberculosis and Malaria, the Global Alliance for Vaccines and Immunisation (GAVI), and the President's Emergency Plan for AIDS Relief (PEPFAR), and contributed to setting the health-related MDGs in the early 2000s.

Thus for low-income countries there has been, and continues to be an array of international organisations (including large NGOs that implement human health interventions such as Save The Children, World Vision, and the International Planned Parenthood Federation (IPPF)) that influence the setting of goals in human health. These international organisations often also have competing agendas, which can hamper coordinated delivery of health interventions, as well as stifle local priorities.

The creation of health goals for the MDGs reflects the diversity of parallel, international health initiatives competing for attention at the turn of this century. This resulted in no less than three specific health goals on maternal and child health and infectious diseases, as well as health-related targets in other goals, such as improved sanitation and reduced hunger. Each of the three goals had its own targets and indicators, and its own implementation programme.

Many have observed that top-down vertical programmes such as these, reflecting donor priorities, may have had a disruptive effect on national efforts to strengthen the broader (horizontal) health system by diverting staff and resources, and setting priorities that are not locally relevant. Conspicuously absent were voices from within the low-income countries themselves, whether from governments, civil societies, bodies of health professionals and experts, local industries (often under-developed or subservient to transnational high-income country corporations), media, local communities, or otherwise.

It is also important to recognise that parallel processes of measurement such as the Global Burden of Disease (GBD) studies (Murray et al. 2012a; Murray et al. 2012b), via the risk factors and diseases they choose to measure and their grouping of these into categories, also have an influence on what human health problems are targeted internationally, and consequently, what goals are set.

There are different approaches to quantifying human health in different countries (e.g. quality adjusted life years (QALY) in the UK (NICE 2008) and other high-income countries), and in sectors such as the insurance industry. But as a global goal setter, the GBD measure stands out, and also provides the 1990 baseline estimates for the MDGs, therefore perhaps also influencing the MDGs goal-setting process. Again as with the policy goal agenda outlined above, the voices of low-income country governments, organisations, and citizens are absent from this process. Poor quality or absence of data from low-income settings can also hamper appropriate priority setting.

What progress has been achieved in this sector through the Millennium Development Goals and other processes?

Through the MDGs, or at least according to the MDGs targets, human health has improved. There are measured reductions in child and infant mortality: MDG 4 (Reduce child mortality) is on track in some of the high-priority countries, and deaths in children under five have declined from approximately 12 million in 1990 to 6.3 million in 2013 (Wang H, Liddell CA, Coates MM, et al. 2014). Reductions are also recorded in maternal mortality, and although MDG 5 (Improve maternal health) is not on track, maternal deaths have nevertheless dropped from approximately 543,000 a year in 1990 to 287,000 in 2010 (Lozano et al. 2011; WHO & UNICEF 2012). A reduction in the incidence of new HIV infections and recent large expansion of antiretroviral treatment for AIDS, as well as a reduction in cases of active tuberculosis (though multidrug resistant tuberculosis is an emerging threat) and in deaths of children under five from malaria (WHO Global Malaria Programme 2013), collectively mean that MDG 6 (Combat HIV/AIDS, malaria, and other diseases) is mainly on track. Many other areas of human health measured by the GBD study, in particular communicable diseases such as lower respiratory infections and diarrhoeal diseases, nutritional deficiencies, and chronic respiratory diseases, also appear to be improving (Murray et al. 2012b). Given that these diseases were not included in the MDGs targets, it is likely that other processes such as demographic shifts and improvements in living standards have been as, or more important to progress in human health than the MDGs.

We should also recognise that non-communicable diseases related to lifestyle factors, pollution, and industrialisation (e.g. trauma from road traffic accidents) are on the rise in many areas of the world. Given these were also not included in the MDGs targets, the narrow focus of the MDGs may have contributed to overlooking such emerging issues.

The most notable processes specifically aimed at improving human health are perhaps increased investment in health systems by governments via donor funding, taxation, and most recently, health insurance. The Abuja Declaration of 2001, which generated a commitment to allocate 15 per cent of government spending to health, although with limited success, may have been a catalyst for such increased funding. It is also possible, however, that along with the large increase in donor funding for health, such improvements have been partially driven by the MDGs agenda.

MDGs 8 (Develop a global partnership for development) and 1 (Eradicate extreme poverty and hunger), respectively, contain goals related to improved sanitation and reduced hunger and are therefore also related to human health. However, they have been less identified with specific health outcomes, less championed, and less achieved than the 'health' MDGs (MDGs 4–6). In some regions, for example Africa, increases in food availability based mostly on cereal production or through food aid have not been followed by improved statistics on nutrition, with stunting still persisting in many countries and nutrition security remaining a critical need. MDG 6 in particular, can be said to have had greater ownership by powerful groupings such as The Global Fund to Fight AIDS, Tuberculosis and Malaria, the PEPFAR, and the BMGF, who introduced the issue onto low-income country agendas ahead of competing priorities in health and other sectors (United Nations 2008).

We should also recognise that there are other aspects of human health (e.g. mental well-being) not included or well accounted for in the MDGs or GBD for which we do not have agreed measures, and for which we can therefore not determine progress. In the last chapter of this book, we focus particularly on the important links between education and sexual and reproductive health (SRH), initially neglected in the MDGs, with its important implications for population growth and wellbeing.

What is the current debate about future goal setting?

The main issues in the debate about future goal setting in human health concern broadening the horizon of goals to include concepts such as universal health coverage, the continuum of care, the life-course approach to health services provision integration, and convergence towards minimum global standards in absolute terms, everywhere. The High-Level Panel of Eminent Persons on the Post-2015 Development Agenda has already drafted human health targets relating to preventing deaths in children under five, ensuring maternal mortality below a set level, increasing vaccination coverage to a minimum level, ensuring universal sexual and reproductive rights, and reducing the burden of key infectious, neglected, and non-communicable diseases (High-Level Panel of Eminent Persons 2014). The Sustainable Development Solutions Network's main goal is to return to the idea of universal access to primary health services, which they believe should include access to services for the prevention and treatment of both non-communicable and communicable diseases, reproductive and sexual health services, pre- and post-natal care, and skilled birth attendance (Sustainable Development Solutions Network 2014). However, the use of evidence and the power and politics behind goal setting must also be considered (Buse & Hawkes 2013).

Strengthening health systems is gaining traction, with the idea that goals related to the improvement of key health system building blocks need to be achieved in order to allow specific health-related goals to be attained (Freedman et al. 2005). These building blocks include: training and retaining enough human resources for health; buying and distributing adequate and affordable stocks of drugs, supplies, and equipment; building and maintaining adequate health facilities at primary, secondary, and tertiary levels; having an adequate health information system with two-way feedback; and having adequate management and financing to ensure cost-effective and responsive services (WHO 2010). However, sufficiently improving health systems is a long-term endeavour, and requires sustained investment over decades. It therefore does not easily lend itself to the setting of goals that are easily achievable or digestible over short time frames.

Equity is also an increasingly important consideration. Measuring the coverage of key maternal, neonatal, and child health (MNCH) interventions for each wealth quintile and the disparity between them has been a recent focus of the Countdown to 2015 initiative, evaluating progress towards MDGs 4 and 5 (Countdown to 2015 (2014)). However, some fear the bottom 10 per cent are not even measured in such assessments of equity, and should be the real focus of future goals, given that current efforts to focus on easier-to-reach populations can increase inequality. Emerging from the recent Global Health 2035 report (Jamison et al. 2013), the idea of Grand Convergence aims for 16-8-4: an under-five mortality rate of 16 per 1,000 live births, an annual AIDS death rate of eight per 100,000 people, and an annual death rate from tuberculosis of four per 100,000 people (Lancet 2014). Such targets necessarily require equity between countries to increase as they converge on similar mortality rates. There are also calls to mainstream consideration of persons with disability, who comprise 15 per cent of the population (United Nations 2013; WHO 2011), by integrating services for people with disabilities into all health systems.

Debates also abound as to how to conceptualise health and health-related goals. On the one hand, there are many stakeholders who would like to see the work on the current health-related MDGs on maternal and child survival and on reducing AIDS, tuberculosis and malaria, finished. There are also those who would like to see goals set on non-communicable diseases, such as ischaemic heart disease, diabetes, stroke, and cancer, which together make up significant burdens of ill health as defined by the GBD study (Murray et al. 2012b; Buse & Hawkes 2013). On the other hand, some stakeholders would like to see a shift away from the narrow definitions of health favoured by clinical medicine towards the broader (and also preventive as well as curative) foci of public health and global health; and would like to see goals related to more holistic understandings of health. Indeed, many conceptualise health as mental and physical, as well as social and environmental, and would like to see concepts such as quality of life, well-being, or health-related capabilities used in goal setting. These concepts, which require qualitative as well as quantitative investigation, are all very difficult to measure, and are perhaps therefore less likely to become future goals. Nevertheless, they are more relevant to integrating human health with other spheres that also impact on quality of life, well-being, and capabilities, and many would like to see such integration reflected in future goal setting. Others argue, however, that simple pre-existing goals such as reducing the under-five mortality rate already capture a lot of complexity and constitute cross-cutting indicators of success for human health and many other important spheres (Hulme 2013).

Calls to broaden the health sphere beyond human health are also being made. The One Health Initiative calls for an integration of human, animal, and environmental (ecosystem) health (Kaplan, Kahn & Monath 2009). The Rio+20 summit has also fostered calls for joint consideration of the linkages between and the integration of 'ecosystem processes, anthropogenic environmental changes (climate change, biodiversity loss, and land use), socio-economic changes, and global health' (Langlois et al. 2012. p.381). Perhaps soon 'planetary health' will supersede 'global health' (Haines, Whitmee & Horton 2014).

The methods of achieving future goals in human health are of course also crucial, and are also subject to intense debate. Most notable is the debate surrounding the extent to which future goals should be nationally led and reflect local country-specific priorities and standards, verses how much they should continue to be donor-led 'global priorities', and how much less-powerful and less-rich voices from the global South should be heeded in setting global priorities (Hulme 2013). Shifts in finance as well as in politics are key here. Tax- and insurance-based systems may be more sustainable, but also require greater democracy and accountability to work properly. Paradoxically, such greater accountability may only occur via reduced dependence on external forces, such as donor governments and institutions.

Although nationally led prioritisation is vital, it is also worth noting that global standardisation is critical to retain and secure the equitable protection of health and rights. There is a danger that governments will ignore or actively suppress morally, socially, or religiously contested issues such as abortion or lesbian, gay, bisexual, and transgender (LGBT) rights, or will restrict access to health resources for certain political, ethnic, or social groups for political reasons; this danger is more prevalent, although not exclusive to countries without established democracies.

The current draft proposal of the Open Working Group for Sustainable Development Goals (OWG 2014) addresses human health directly in only one of 17 goals. However, this goal (Ensure healthy lives and promote well-being for all at all ages) has nine numbered sub-goals, with targets covering everything from the subjects of the existing health MDGs to non-communicable diseases, mental health, substance abuse, road traffic accidents, family planning, universal health coverage, and pollution. Four additional lettered sub-goals are also included on tobacco, access to medicines, health workers, and early warning systems. Health will be affected by many of the other 16 goals, including those related to poverty, hunger, water and sanitation, the environment, inequality, and cities. With 17 goals and hundreds of targets, clearly this is an agenda far more ambitious than the MDGs. What its final form will take, including how targets will be set for the numerous sub-goals that are so far only vaguely defined, and how far it will be delivered given the complexities discussed above, remains to be seen.

References

Buse, K., & S. Hawkes. (2013). Health post-2015: evidence and power. *Lancet*. Published online 20 September 2013.

Freedman, L. P., Waldman, R. J., de Pinho, H., Wirth, M. E., Chowdhury, M. A. R., & Rosenfield, A. (2005). Transforming health systems to improve the lives of women and children. *Lancet, 365*, 997–1000.

Haines, A., Whitmee, S., & Horton, R. (2014). Planetary health: a call for papers. *Lancet, 384*, 379–380.

High-Level Panel of Eminent Persons. (2014). *Goal 4: Ensure Healthy Lives* (The report of the high-level panel of eminent persons on the post-2015 development agenda). New York: United Nations.

Hulme, D. (2013). The Post-2015 Development Agenda: Learning from the MDGs. Southern Voice Occasional Paper 2. Dhaka, Bangladesh: Centre for Policy Dialogue.

Jamison, D. T., Summers, L. H., Alleyne, G., Arrow, K. J., Berkley, S., Binagwaho, A., Bustreo, F., et al. (2013). Global Health 2035: a world converging within a generation. *Lancet, 382*, 1898–1955.

Kaplan, B., Kahn, L. H., & Monath, T. P. (2009). One Health-One Medicine: linking human, animal and environmental health [whole special issue]. *Veterinaria Italiana, 45*(1).

Lancet (Editorial). (2014). Grand convergence: a future sustainable development goal? *Lancet, 383*, 187.

Langlois, E. V., Campbell, K., Prieur-Richard, A. H., Karesh, W. B., & Daszak, P. (2012). Towards a better integration of global health and biodiversity in the new sustainable development goals beyond Rio+20. *Ecohealth, 9*(4), 381–385.

Lozano, R., Wang, H., Foreman, K. J., Rajaratnam, J. K., Naghavi, M., Marcus, J. R., Dwyer-Lindgren, L., et al. (2011). Progress towards Millennium Development Goals 4 and 5 on maternal and child mortality: an updated systematic analysis. *Lancet, 378*, 1139–1165.

Murray, C. J. L., Ezzati, M., Flaxman, A. D., Lim, S., Lozano, R., Michaud, C., Naghavi, M., et al. (2012a). GBD 2010: design, definitions, and metrics. *Lancet, 380*, 2063–2066.

Murray, C. J. L., Vos, T., Lozano, R., Naghavi, M., Flaxman, A. D., Michaud, C., Ezzati, M., et al. (2012b). Disability-adjusted life years (DALYs) for 291 diseases and injuries in 21 regions, 1990-2010: a systematic analysis for the Global Burden of Disease Study 2010. *Lancet, 380*, 2197–2223.

National Institute for Health and Clinical Excellence (NICE). (2008). Guide to the methods of technology appraisal. London: National Institute of Clinical Excellence.

Open Working Group. (2014). *Proposal for Sustainable Development Goals.* Retrieved from https://sustainabledevelopment.un.org/focussdgs.html

Sustainable Development Solutions Network. (2014). *Health for All. Sustainable Development Solutions Network. A Global Initiative for the United Nations.* Retrieved from http://unsdsn.org/what-we-do/thematic-groups/health-for-all/

United Nations. (2008). Delivering on the global partnership for achieving the millennium development goals. MDG Gap Task Force Report. New York: United Nations.

United Nations. (2013). *Outcome document of the high-level meeting of the General Assembly on the realisation of the Millennium Development Goals and other internationally agreed development goals for people with disabilities: the way forward, a disability-inclusive development agenda towards 2015 and beyond.* A/RES/68/3. Retrieved from http://www.un.org/disabilities/default.asp?id=1590

Wang H, Liddell CA, Coates MM, et al. (2014). Global, regional, and national levels of neonatal, infant, and under-5 mortality during 1990–2013: a systematic analysis for the Global Burden of Disease Study 2013. *The Lancet* 2014; 384(9947): 957–79.

World Health Organization (WHO). (2010). Key components of a well-functioning health system. Geneva, Switzerland: WHO.

World Health Organization (WHO). (2011). *World Report on Disability.* Geneva, Switzerland: WHO.

World Health Organization (WHO) Global Malaria Programme. (2013). World Malaria Report. Geneva, Switzerland: WHO.

World Health Organization (WHO) & United Nations International Children's Emergency Fund (UNICEF). (2014). *Countdown to 2015, maternal, newborn and child survival: fulfilling the Health Agenda for Women and Children, the 2014 report.* Retrieved from http://www.healthynewbornnetwork.org/sites/default/files/resources/Countdown_to_2015-Fulfilling%20the%20Health_Agenda_for_Women_and_Children-The_2014_Report-Conference_Draft.pdf

Population growth

Susannah H. Mayhew[*] and Tim Colbourn[†]

[*]London School of Hygiene and Tropical Medicine, Department of Global Health and Development, [†]University College London, Institute for Global Health

What is the historical process by which goal setting in this sector has developed?

Population movement has a long and political history, with goal setting linked at various times to macro-economic and development decisions, women's health, conservative religious agendas, and individual rights.

Since the 1950s, demographics has been seen as a core consideration of economic development. Overpopulation and rapid population growth were seen as major barriers to economic growth (Coale & Hoover 1958), sometimes linked to more Malthusian concerns about overreaching the Earth's human carrying capacity (Ehrlich 1968; Meadows et al. 1972). This led many developing countries to invest in the procurement and distribution of commercially accessible contraception throughout the 1950s and 60s, in order to secure economic progress. Formal government family planning programmes were established in many developing countries over the next three decades. The development of NGOs also proliferated: the IPPF was founded in 1952 and the UNFPA was founded in 1969. Family planning programmes tended to focus on limiting numbers of births among married women. In some parts of the world (notably India and China) this narrow approach led, in some cases, to coercive practices that tainted the entire population agenda with the spectre of population control, and even eugenics. In India, the forced sterilisation programme of the mid 1970s brought down a Government. In China,

How to cite this book chapter:
Mayhew, S. H. and Colbourn, T. 2015. Population growth. In: Waage, J and Yap, C. (eds.) *Thinking Beyond Sectors for Sustainable Development*. Pp. 37–44. London: Ubiquity Press. DOI: http://dx.doi.org/10.5334/bao.e

the one-child policy and aggressive promotion of long-acting contraceptives initiated in 1978 brought many millions of people out of poverty; however, this was at the expense of abuses of individual rights (especially of women), including forced abortions, sterilisations, and a wide range of severe socio-economic penalties. Population programmes became politically toxic and family planning was relegated to a mere women's health issue.

During the late 1980s and early 1990s, a broad coalition of women's health and rights groups emerged which collectively gained experience in lobbying the United Nations agencies tasked with sexual and reproductive health and rights (SRHR) issues. They were fighting (particularly through the United Nations conference processes) for a move away from equating reproductive issues solely with fertility control, to encompass a more holistic approach to people's SRH needs (Dixon-Mueller 1993; Sen, Germain & Chen 1994). At the same time the rise of HIV was attracting substantial attention, and its link with a range of other sexually transmitted infections (STIs) led to a broad consensus on the need to tackle such diseases together with reproductive services as part of a more holistic approach. These changes in attitude and approach crystallised at the International Conference on Population and Development (ICPD) in Cairo in 1994. The resulting 20-year Programme of Action was a paradigm shift, embracing a reproductive health agenda built around health, choice, and rights. This approach was reinforced a year later by the Beijing Declaration from the Fourth International Conference on Women in Beijing in 1995, which reaffirmed reproductive rights as basic human rights. In practice, however, the complex and diffuse ICPD agenda was hard to implement, with no clear targets, and resulted in a narrowing of the focus to integration of STI/HIV and family planning/reproductive health services, adolescent SRH, and a general neglect of funding for family planning services. In effect, this progressive agenda was delinked from demographic issues, partly because it was felt important to create an agenda that distanced itself from those policies and programmes which had sometimes been associated with coercive practices (Blanc & Tsui 2005).

As a result of the ICPD, governments and donors throughout the developing world have pursued a multi-pronged approach to SRHR. This has led to difficulties in prioritisation and resourcing, and has sometimes meant that inappropriate priorities have been pursued to the detriment of family planning investment; for example, a narrow focus on HIV and maternal health targets rather than tackling urgent underlying issues such as adolescent sexuality and health needs and unsafe abortion (Mayhew & Adjei 2004).

Subsequently, funding for family planning declined significantly, while that for HIV treatment increased exponentially. This was associated with the religiously conservative Bush administration in the US during the 2000s, with its opposition to aspects of contraceptive programmes, abortion, and other SRH and rights issues. As a result, UNFPA took the decision not to hold its usual decennial Population Conference, for fear of having the progressive ICPD Programme of Action retracted. In fact, the 1994 ICPD was the last such global conference to take place. Many developing countries saw a slowing and even stalling of the decline in their fertility rates during this period, as well as regression in other health indicators, such as immunisation rates, as population growth increased and public health services struggled to keep up with rapidly increasing populations of children (Bryce et al. 2005). Global population increased from about 5.6 billion in 1994 to more than seven billion in 2015, with the most rapid growth occurring in sub-Saharan Africa. Yet development priorities for health gradually shifted away from population (family planning) towards HIV, while population became incorporated within the broad SRH agenda, rather than being seen as a development issue in its own right.

By the time the MDGs goals and targets were being negotiated, population fell under the remit of the SRH practitioners who had an uneasy relationship with the topic, many wanting to distance themselves from any perceived association with coercion. As a result, they largely failed to see the significance of the MDGs agenda, neglecting to engage in the necessary lobbying to secure SRHR targets within these influential goals. Eventually, after a protracted period of catch-up lobbying, SRHR targets (specifically on achieving universal access to reproductive health, for which various indicators were incorporated) were added and finally accepted in 2008. The lack of demographic or reproductive health goals or targets for so long within the MDGs has led to another de-emphasis of population dynamics on development prospects (Bernstein 2005; Crossette 2005; United Nations Millennium Project 2006).

More recently, however, population issues have been returning to the development discourse within the UK and beyond. More recent reassessments of the impact of demographic trends on economic outcomes have also (re)confirmed that fertility decline (as well as female education and labour force participation) is linked with better economic prospects (Bloom, Canning & Malaney 2000; Eastwood & Lipton 1999; Mammen & Paxson 2000).

In 2006 the UK Government's All Party Parliamentary Group on Population, Development and Reproductive Health held a hearing, resulting in the report *Return of the Population Growth Factor* (All Parliamentary Group on Population, Development and Reproductive Health 2007). Three years later, the DFID reinstated dedicated funding for research on family planning (alongside abortion), and in 2012 the BMGF held the London Summit on Family Planning, jointly hosted with the DFID, pledging increased funding for family planning and creating the FP2020 global partnership to advance family planning. Concomitant with this, other population dynamics including demographic trends related to urbanisation, migration, ageing, and household composition, as well as population growth, are increasingly being discussed as part of the international development discourse.

What progress has been achieved in this sector through the Millennium Development Goals and other processes?

Stabilisation of population growth did not benefit directly or significantly from the MDGs since it was not until 2008 that Target 5B on universal access to SRH, which included measures of contraceptive prevalence rate and unmet need for family planning (i.e. women wishing to stop or delay childbearing but who are not using contraception), was finally adopted. As discussed above, population growth is a very sensitive political issue, and since the 1994 ICPD Programme of Action family planning has suffered declining funding and political commitment, which has affected progress on the fertility indicators.

The global commitment to reducing population growth rates from the 1950s contributed to a decline in global total fertility rates (births per woman) for several decades, although in the same time period the world population doubled from three to six billion as a result of population momentum (i.e. the tendency for population growth to continue beyond the time that replacement level fertility has been achieved because of the relatively high concentration of people in their childbearing years). In 2013 the world's population growth rate had slowed from its peak of two per cent per year in the 1960s to 1.1 per cent in 2013, and fertility in Asia and Latin America had dropped from over five births per woman to 2.2. On the whole, those countries and regions where information and contraceptives were made available saw a moderate to rapid decline in the birth rate. In addition, there was an improvement in the economy, the health of women and their families, and the autonomy, education, and status of women. The countries where many pregnancies remained unwanted and the birth rate did not fall are often seeing a growth of urban slums, a failure of the state to keep pace with educational demands and, in some cases, continuing oppression of women.

Since the MDGs were agreed in 2000 the pace of decline has slowed, and in some countries in sub-Saharan Africa it has stalled entirely, even in the few countries like Kenya where fertility decline seemed well established (Bongaarts 2008; Ezeh, Mberu & Emima 2009). Today in sub-Saharan Africa, the total fertility rate (births per woman) is 5.1 compared to 4.1 across all least developed countries (LDCs), and 2.6 among less developed countries (UNFPA 2013). The official United Nations estimates of global population projections have been creeping upwards over the last decade. Assuming current rates of fertility decline are maintained, the world population of 7.2 billion in mid-2013 is projected to increase by almost one billion people within the next 12 years, reaching 8.1 billion in 2025, and to further increase to 9.6 billion in 2050, and 10.9 billion by 2100 (United Nations Department of Economic and Social Affairs 2013).

The fertility indicators in the MDGs are included in MDG 5A (Reduce by three quarters, between 1990 and 2015, the maternal mortality ratio)). This is the MDG on which least progress has been made. Although it is not possible to draw a causal link, it is quite plausible that the stubborn rate of decline in maternal mortality, particularly in countries with the highest fertility, has something to do with the politicisation of contraception that has affected the funding and delivery of contraceptive programmes over the last decade and a half. As well as being the slowest of the MDGs to improve, maternal mortality also shows the greatest disparity between rich and poor countries. It is no coincidence that sub-Saharan Africa has by far the highest maternal mortality ratio of any region (currently 500 out of 100,000 live births compared to 240 out of 100,000 for all developing country regions together), and also has the highest levels of unmet need for family planning (25 per cent compared to 13 per cent for all developing country regions) (United Nations 2013). Not surprisingly, maternal mortality in Africa tends to be lower in countries where levels of contraceptive use and skilled attendance at birth are relatively high. Indeed, the contribution of contraception to maternal mortality reduction globally is large. Estimates from 2008 show that the use of modern methods of contraception in developing countries was responsible for averting 230,000 maternal deaths, equivalent to a 43 per cent reduction, and much larger numbers of abortions and miscarriages were also averted (Singh et al. 2009).

Globally the education of girls, women's employment, and greater gender equity have influenced contraceptive uptake and desire for smaller family sizes among both women and men. The availability of new technologies through exposure to global debate on issues such as fertility and gender empowerment have also had an impact on increasing demand for and use of contraception. The 2013 MDGs Report shows that the use of mobile phones and the internet has increased very significantly during the 2000s, but we know nothing about the gendered make-up of this. By 2015, total demand for family planning among married women is projected to grow to more than 900 million, mostly due to population growth (United Nations 2013). Yet donor funding for family planning has occupied an ever decreasing proportion of population assistance. In 1999, family planning accounted for 37 per cent of the total global donor expenditure on population activities, while HIV/AIDS received 23 per cent. By 2009, HIV/AIDS received 68 per cent of the total population expenditure (despite declining since 2007), while family planning received only seven per cent (UNFPA 2011).

What is the current debate about future goal setting?

Today, population and family planning appear to be coming back onto donors' agendas, though still largely in relation to health. The 2012 London Summit on Family Planning and its associated spin-off activities has created probably the most influential donor forum for family planning-related global goal setting. The WHO's universal health coverage call has dominated its own global goal-setting negotiations, and UNFPA continues to track the standard demographic targets collected by the Demographic and Health Surveys Program around the world, as well as donor funding for population assistance, but has not strongly lobbied for their inclusion in the post-2015 goals and targets.

The SRHR civil society community that was so influential at the ICPD in Cairo is also re-engaging with the international post-2015 goal-setting negotiations to secure a target of universal access to SRH in the SDGs presented. Although they may be more engaged than other specific health communities, the voices of SRHR advocates are more fragmented than they were at the Cario ICPD (partly reflecting the continuing lack of consensus over the primacy of population issues versus the wide range of other SRHR goals arising from Cairo).

During the months before the 2009 United Nations Climate Change Conference in Copenhagen, the Population and Climate Change Alliance (a loose grouping of northern and southern NGOs working to increase awareness of the links between population dynamics and climate change) was formed to interact with the climate change and wider sustainable development discourse, building on new research on the linkages between population dynamics and climate change (Bryant et al. 2009). This network, now named the Population and Sustainable Development Alliance (PSDA), has been critical in securing small steps to reconnect population issues with sustainable development, including lobbying at the Rio+20 Summit negotiations and securing language on sexual and reproductive health, as well as a Health and Population section in the outcome document which notes 'Through forward looking planning, we can seize the opportunities and address the challenges associated with demographic change.' (UN General Assembly Resolution 66/288: para 144:28)). PSDA are also monitoring subsequent commitments. Most notably, perhaps, health and population dynamics were included on the agenda of the Fourth Session of the Open Working Group on Sustainable Development Goals meeting in 2013, and population dynamics was the theme of one of the 11 post-2015 United Nations thematic consultations and in April 2015 the UN Commission on Population and Development's 48th Session debated "integrating population issues into sustainable development, including in the post-2015 development agenda" (UN Commission on Population and Development 2015).

References

All Parliamentary Group on Population, Development and Reproductive Health. (2007, January). *Return of the Population Growth Factor: Its impact upon the Millennium Development Goals* (Report of Hearings by the All Party Parliamentary Group on Population, Development and Reproductive Health). London: House of Commons.

Bernstein, S. (2005). The changing discourse on population and development: toward a new political demography. *Studies in Family Planning, 36*(2), 127–132.

Blanc, A. K., & Tsui, A. O. (2005). The dilemma of past successes: insiders' views on the future of the International Family Planning Movement. *Studies in Family Planning*, *36*(4), 263–276.

Bloom, D. E., Canning, D., & Malaney, P. N. (2000). Population dynamics and economic growth in Asia. *Population and Development Review*, *26*, Supplement: Population and Economic Change in East Asia (2000), 257–290.

Bongaarts, J. (2008). Fertility transitions in developing countries: progress or stagnation? *Studies in Family Planning*, *39*(2), 105–110.

Bryant, L., Carver, L., Butler, C. D., & Anage, A. (2009). Climate change and family planning: least-developed countries define the agenda. *Bull World Health Organ*, *87*, 852–857.

Bryce, J., Black, R. E., Walker, N., Bhutta, Z. A., Lawn, J. E., & Steketee, R. W. (2005). Can the world afford to save the lives of 6 million children each year? *Lancet*, *365*, 2193–2200.

Coale, A. J., & Hoover, E. M. (1958). Population growth and economic development in low-income countries. Princeton: Princeton University Press.

Crossette, B. (2005). Reproductive health and the Millennium Development Goals: the missing link. *Studies in Family Planning*, *36*(1), 71–79.

Dixon-Mueller, R. (1993). Population policy and women's rights: transforming reproductive choice. Westport, USA: Praeger Publishers.

Eastwood, R., & Lipton, M. (1999). The impact of changes in human fertility on poverty. *Journal of Development Studies*, *36* (1), 1–30.

Ehrlich, P. (1968). The population bomb. New York: Buccaneer Books.

Ezeh, A. C., Mberu, B. U., & Emima, J. O. (2009). Stall in fertility decline in eastern African countries: regional analysis of patterns, determinants and implications. *Philosophical Transactions of the Royal Society B, 364* (1532).

Mammen, K., & Paxson, C. (2000). Women's work and economic development. *Journal of Economic Perspectives*, *14*(4), 141–164.

Mayhew, S. H., & Adjei, S. (2004). Sexual and reproductive health: challenges for priority-setting in Ghana's health reforms. *Health Policy and Planning*, *19*, i50–i61.

Meadows, D. H., Meadows, D. L, Randers, J., & Behrens III, W. W. (1972). The limits to growth. New York: Mentor and Plume Books.

Newman K., Fisher S., Mayhew S., Stephenson J. (2014) Population, sexual and reproductive health, rights and sustainable development: forging a common agenda. *Reproductive Health Matters* 22(43):53–64. DOI: http://dx.doi.org/10.1016/S0968-8080(14)43770-4

Sen, G., Germain, A., & Chen, L. C. (Eds.) (1994). Population policies reconsidered: health, empowerment and rights. Boston, Massachusetts: Harvard Centre for Population and Development Studies.

Singh, S., Wulf, D., Hussain, R., Bankole, A., & Sedgh, G. (2009). Abortion worldwide: a decade of uneven progress. New York: Guttmacher Institute.

United Nations. (2013). The Millennium Development Goals Report 2013. New York: United Nations.

United Nations Commission on Population and Development (2015). Retrieved from   http://www.un.org/en/development/desa/population/commission/sessions/2015/index.shtml

United Nations, Department of Economic and Social Affairs. (2013). World population prospects: the 2012 revision, key findings and advance tables. Working Paper No. ESA/P/WP.227. New York: United Nations.

United Nations Millennium Project. (2006). Public choices, private decisions: sexual and reproductive health and the millennium development goals. Geneva, Switzerland: United Nations.

United Nations Population Fund (UNFPA). (2011). Financial resource flows for population activities in 2009. New York: UNFPA.

United Nations Population Fund (UNFPA). (2013). The demography of adaptation to climate change. London: UNFPA and International Institute for Environment and Development.

Agriculture and food

Yoseph Araya[*], Andrew Dorward[†], Jasmine Gideon[*], Richard Kock[‡], Laurence Smith[§] and Jeff Waage[¶]

[*]Birkbeck College, Department of Geography, Environment and Development Studies, [†]School of Oriental and African Studies, Centre for Environment, Development and Policy, [*]Birkbeck College, Department of Geography, Environment and Development Studies, [‡]Royal Veterinary College, Department of Pathology and Pathogen Biology, [§]School of Oriental and African Studies, Centre for Development, Environment and Policy, [¶]London International Development Centre; School of Oriental and African Studies, Centre for Development, Environment and Policy

What is the historical process by which goal setting in this sector has developed?

Over the past two decades, there has been little development in goal setting directed specifically at targets and indicators for agriculture and food outcomes. This reflects the limited attention given by the international development community to agriculture in the late 1990s and early 2000s. The FAO's 2002 World Food Summit, which aimed to boost the disappointing progress made five years after the 1996 Summit, reiterated the earlier pledge to reduce the number of hungry people to 400 million by 2015. African Heads of Government did, however, agree to allocate 10 per cent of their national budgets to agriculture in the 2003 Maputo Declaration. Since the publication of the *World Development Report 2008: Agriculture for Development* and the 2008 global food price spike, a renewed interest in agriculture has led to generally unfulfilled budgetary and spending commitments (e.g. the 2009 G8

How to cite this book chapter:
Araya, Y, Dorward, A, Gideon, J, Kock, R, Smith, L, and Waage, J. 2015. Agriculture and food. In: Waage, J and Yap, C. (eds.) *Thinking Beyond Sectors for Sustainable Development*. Pp. 45–50. London: Ubiquity Press. DOI: http://dx.doi.org/10.5334/bao.f

'*L'Aquila*' *Joint Statement on Global Food Security* and subsequent G8 meetings), however, to date no achievement targets have been agreed.

Agriculture and food-related outcomes were embedded in MDG 1(Eradicate Extreme poverty and hunger), which included hunger targets (Target 1C, 'Halve, between 1990 and 2015, the proportion of people who suffer from hunger') and indicators (1.8, 'Prevalence of underweight children under-five years of age', and 1.9, 'Proportion of population below minimum level of dietary energy consumption'). The MDG 1.9 indicator was based on the 1996 World Food Summit goal of reducing the number of people suffering from hunger by half by 2015. The process of deciding these targets involved different constituencies engaged with the two different indicators.

UNICEF, the WHO, and a range of governments and other agencies have been responsible for providing data on the prevalence of underweight children under five years of age (indicator 1.8) through surveys using, or compatible with, UNICEF's Multiple Indicator Cluster Survey (MICS), including the USAID-supported Demographic and Health Surveys programme. Although performance on this indicator is significantly related to food security (defined in terms of access to food, and its nutritional quality and utilisation), hunger itself (defined in terms of access to food) is more closely associated with indicator 1.9. FAO has published data on indicator 1.9, but there have been methodological and data difficulties that make it a poor measure of hunger or food insecurity. Concerns about this in the wake of the 2008 food price spike led to major methodological revisions by the FAO in 2012 (FAO, WFP & IFAD 2012). While the new method has a number of improvements, there are still a number of concerns (for example the data is often poor and only looks at nutrition in terms of calories). There are also difficulties with indicator 1.8, as data is not available on an annual basis and stunting and wasting are better indicators of the separate effects of more chronic and acute undernutrition.

There has been little consideration of natural or wild food systems beyond consideration of their sustainability and governance, though some of these are locally and/or globally important for food security, most notably capture fisheries. Addressing potential negative effects of agriculture, including environmental degradation and the risk of food-related and zoonotic diseases, have also not figured directly in the development of goal setting.

What progress has been achieved in this sector through the Millennium Development Goals and other processes?

With regards to indicator 1.8, the global target does not look like it will be met, with mixed achievements in different parts of Asia, non-achievement in Africa, and achievement in Latin America and the Caribbean.

With regards to indicator 1.9, a similar pattern is observed, with revised estimates showing that falls in the prevalence of undernourished people prior to 2007 were not quite sufficient to be on track for meeting the MDG 1 target, and food price increases in 2008 and subsequent years further slowed down the rate of fall in incidence. However, with population growth in most poor and food insecure countries, absolute numbers of undernourished people have hardly fallen, meaning that the World Food Summit global target of halving the number of hungry people from that in 1990–92 by 2015 will be missed by a very wide margin.

As with other MDGs targets, there are wide variations between regions as regards to changes in prevalence and numbers of undernourished people. FAO, World Food Programme (WFP), and the International Fund for Agricultural Development (IFAD) (2013) estimates that absolute numbers of undernourished people have been falling in Asia, Latin America, and the Caribbean, with falls in prevalence on track to meet the MDGs target. In both West Asia and sub-Saharan Africa, however, absolute numbers of undernourished people have been rising, with some falls in prevalence in sub-Saharan Africa, but actual increases in prevalence in West Asia; although this is from a much lower 1990–92 starting point than that the other regions. Within Asia there has been a remarkable fall in prevalence in South East Asia, with a slightly lower but still remarkable fall in East Asia. However, South Asia achieved a lower fall in prevalence which, if continued, will not be enough to achieve the target. These reductions have, however, been achieved at considerable environmental cost and hence threats to their sustainability in the context of continuing economic and population growth. Fisheries management and stocks have fallen, though in some cases harvesting has been sustained by increases in fishing efforts. Zoonotic disease outbreaks and spread have increased.

What is the current debate about future goal setting?

Food and agriculture system debates are dominated by concerns about food security and sustainability. Food security is considered in terms of four pillars: availability, access and entitlements, utilisation, and stability. The goal-setting agenda tends to only explicitly consider the first two of these (sustainable food production and availability and access). Nutrition (which should encompass all four pillars) is often considered separately. Discussions of sustainable production, of access, and of nutrition all include issues of stability. However, whilst a variety of indicators (of varying quality) have been developed for measuring food availability, access, and utilisation, very few have been explicitly developed and applied to measure stability in any of these dimensions (Pangaribow, Gerber & Torero 2013). Consequently, FAO, WFP, and IFAD (2013) and Pangaribow, Gerber & Torero (2013) set out a wide range of potential indicators for the four pillars of food security, considering the relationships between the indicators and the pillars they describe, and the way that these change according to the scale of analysis (e.g. global, regional, national, sub-national groups, households, and individuals within households).

Sustainability concerns tend to focus most attention on the sustainability of food production systems and therefore on food availability, revolving around the effects of population and economic growth on food demands (with economic growth leading to increased demand for more resource demanding livestock products), and resource loss and degradation (including the effects of climate change) depressing supply. Overall (global) supply capacities tend to be the focus of more technical agricultural debates.

Regional differences in supply and demand lead to considerations of regional food access, but there are also concerns about access for vulnerable groups (e.g. marginalised rural poor or deprived urban migrants, in terms of access and forced dietary change). Issues also arise around the nature of malnutrition, with important distinctions between undernutrition (shortage of calories), the increasing incidence of over-nutrition (leading to obesity and non-communicable diseases), and 'hidden hunger' from shortages of micronutrients, of which there are complex interactions between the three.

In the wider delineation the Open Working Group proposal *Introduction and Proposed Goals and Targets on Sustainable Development for the Post-2015 Development Agenda* highlights agriculture and food security, stressing its centrality to sustainable development. The key aspects are addressed in Goal 2 (End hunger, achieve food security and improved nutrition, and promote sustainable agriculture). Here, agriculture and food security are addressed in terms of food availability with brief mentions on food access, nutrition, and stability. However, there is no specific mention of the role of other relevant aspects in attaining agriculture and food security goals, such as gender equality (in Goal 5), healthy nutrition (in Goal 3), sustainable water/natural resource management (in Goals 6 and 15). As in the past, fisheries are considered largely in terms of conservation and governance (Goal 14), not as critical for local or global livelihoods and food systems, although rapid increases in aquaculture production are recognised.

In the 10 proposed Sustainable Development Solutions Network goals (Sustainable Development Solutions Network 2013a), Goal 6 explicitly focuses on increased agricultural productivity and rural prosperity, while Goal 1 focuses on ending poverty, including hunger and malnutrition. However, agriculture and food systems targets are seen as important for a large number of other goals, with a comprehensive discussion of these in *Solutions for Sustainable Agriculture and Food Systems: technical report for the post-205 development agenda* (Sustainable Development Solutions Network 2013b). This stresses the centrality of agriculture and food to other aspects of sustainable development, and argues for the pursuit of agricultural development through 'sustainable intensification', which aims to reduce the environmental footprint of agriculture while meeting all of its other goals.

A relatively new element of the debate on future agriculture and food goals relates to nutrition. While agricultural development has always had an implicit nutritional agenda relating to meeting human needs for energy, expectations on agriculture for nutrition are changing rapidly. An influential Lancet series in 2013 concluded that future nutrition-specific interventions for the poor (e.g. supplementary foods for mothers and infants) could not deliver all the improvements in nutrition (particularly micronutrients) required for healthy development, and that agriculture might play a larger role, e.g. through the increased availability and affordability of animal-based foods, pulses, vegetables, and fruit (Ruel, Alderman & the Maternal and Child Nutrition Study Group 2013). Further, while undernutrition persists in low- and middle-income countries, obesity and other diet-related diseases are growing rapidly as well, and reflecting the same problem: that diets of the poor are dominated by foods high in calories and low in essential micronutrients. The establishment of a Global Panel on Agriculture and Food Systems for Nutrition in 2014 and launch of a Global Nutrition Report, which clearly indicates the important role of agriculture (IFPRI 2014), has stimulated an intense dialogue on how best to embed nutritional outcomes in the agriculture goals of the SDGs.

References

Food and Agriculture Organization of the United Nations (FAO), World Food Programme (WFP), & International Fund for Agricultural Development (IFAD). (2012). The state of food insecurity in the world 2012. Economic growth is necessary but not sufficient to accelerate reduction of hunger and malnutrition. Rome: FAO.

Food and Agriculture Organization of the United Nations (FAO), World Food Programme (WFP), & International Fund for Agricultural Development (IFAD). (2013). The state of food insecurity in the world 2013. The multiple dimensions of food insecurity. Rome: FAO.

International Food Policy Research Institute (IFPRI). (2014). Global nutrition report 2014: actions and accountability to accelerate the world's progress on nutrition. Washington DC: IFPRI.

Pangaribow, E., Gerber, N., & Torero, M. (2013). *Food and nutrition security indicators: a review.* FOODSECURE working paper 5. The Hague: LEI Wageningen UR.

Ruel M., Alderman, H., & the Maternal and Child Nutrition Study Group. (2013). Nutrition-sensitive interventions and programmes: how can they help to accelerate progress in improving maternal and child nutrition? *Lancet,* DOI: http://dx.doi.org/10.1016/S0140-6736(13)60843-0

Sustainable Development Solutions Network. (2013a). An action agenda for sustainable development: report for the UN secretary-general. New York: United Nations.

Sustainable Development Solutions Network. (2013b). Solutions for Sustainable Agriculture and Food Systems: technical report for the post-205 development agenda. New York: United Nations.

UN Open Working Group on Sustainable Development Goals (OWG SDG) (2015) *Introduction and Proposed Goals and Targets on Sustainable Development for the Post2015 Development Agenda. Zero Draft.* New York: United Nations. Retrieved from https://sustainabledevelopment.un.org/content/documents/4523zerodraft.pdf

Education, information, and knowledge

Elaine Unterhalter[*], Nigel Poole[†] and Niall Winters[‡]

*University College London Institute of Education, Department of Humanities and Social Sciences, †School of Oriental and African Studies, Centre for Environment, Development and Policy, ‡University of Oxford, Department of Education

What is the historical process by which goal setting in this sector has developed?

Universal primary education (UPE) was formalised in 2002 as the second MDG (Achieve universal primary education). MDG 2 has one target: to ensure that, by 2015, children everywhere, boys and girls alike, will be able to complete a full course of primary schooling. Three indicators are associated with the target: the net enrolment ratio in primary education for girls and for boys; the proportion of pupils starting grade 1 who reach (rather than complete) grade 5; and the literacy rate of 15–24-year-olds. This narrow focus on enrolment, primary school, and literacy for only one age group represented a significant narrowing of the remit of a wider rights-based formulation of global ambitions with regard to education, which had grown for over half a century.

Some of the focus of MDG 2 can be traced back to the Universal Declaration of Human Rights, which enshrined the right of all to education in 1948. This had a scope that was wider than formal schooling, taking in adult literacy, concerns with equality, and a stress on education for peace. In the 1960s, UNESCO sponsored regional conferences to promote the ideas of universal, compulsory, and free education, with a focus on both primary schooling and adult literacy. A number of rights-based international instruments,

How to cite this book chapter:
Unterhalter, E, Poole, N, and Winters, N. 2015. Education, information, and knowledge. In: Waage, J and Yap, C. (eds.) *Thinking Beyond Sectors for Sustainable Development.* Pp. 51–61. London: Ubiquity Press. DOI: http://dx.doi.org/10.5334/bao.g

sponsored by agencies of the United Nations, expanded discussion of the right to education in the 1970s and 1980s. These focussed on aspects of women's rights, the content of education, and social and economic rights. The adoption of the Convention on the Rights of the Child in 1989, which a large number of governments ratified, paved the way for additional policy momentum on the Education for All (EFA) movement.

The World Conference on Education for All, held in Jomtien, Thailand in March 1990, attended by 4 organisations of the United Nations, 155 governments, and 150 NGOs, was one of the first post-Cold War convening conferences, and adopted the World Declaration on EFA. The vision was of universalising the right to education, with additional stress on forms of exclusion associated with gender, location, and poverty. The UNICEF World Summit on Children, held in New York in September 1990, placed an emphasis on child health and education, identifying a wider range of issues than just UPE, including early childhood development, vocational training, and preparation for employment, and also stressed the importance of developing strategies for measurement and evaluation.

The follow-up EFA conference in Dakar, Senegal in June 2000 identified the development of Education Management Information Systems (EMIS) as a key means to track policy delivery. *The Dakar Framework for Action* (2000) identified six goals:

Goal 1: Expanding and improving comprehensive early childhood care and education, especially for the most vulnerable and disadvantaged children.

Goal 2: Ensuring that by 2015 all children, particularly girls, children in difficult circumstances and those belonging to ethnic minorities, have access to and complete free and compulsory primary education of good quality.

Goal 3: Ensuring that the learning needs of all young people and adults are met through equitable access to appropriate learning and life skills programmes.

Goal 4: Achieving a 50 per cent improvement in levels of adult literacy by 2015, especially for women, and equitable access to basic and continuing education for all adults.

Goal 5: Eliminating gender disparities in primary and secondary education by 2005, and achieving gender equality in education by 2015, with a focus on ensuring girls' full and equal access to and achievement in basic education of good quality.

Goal 6: Improving every aspects of the quality of education, and ensuring their excellence so that recognised and measurable learning outcomes are achieved by all, especially in literacy, numeracy and essential life skills (EFA, 2000).

It can be seen that the target identified under MDG 2, with the stress on UPE, was narrower than the six Dakar EFA Goals. Although MDG 2 had an indicator on measuring young adult literacy, it did not articulate the vision of the Dakar Framework with regard to adult literacy, and did not address the question of quality.

MDG 3 (Promote gender equality and empower women) included a target on gender parity in primary, secondary, and tertiary education. This too, was an attenuation of the vision with regard to gender expressed in the Dakar Framework, which itself was a narrowing of a much broader articulation of goals concerned with gender, education, and women's rights set out in the United Nations Fourth World Conference on Women and the Beijing Declaration of 1995.

What progress has been achieved in this sector through the Millennium Development Goals and other processes?

The formulation of MDG 2 and the six Dakar goals helped mobilise an alliance between international and national policy makers, education activists at a national and international level, and a research community. This grouping is sometimes referred to as the EFA movement (Mundy & Manion 2015). One strand of the EFA movement was concerned with approaches to monitoring progress on the EFA goals and the MDGs. From 2002, UNESCO published an annual *Global Monitoring Report on Education for All* (GMR-EFA), which led the way on governments' data collection systems and contributed to debates emerging about what could and should be measured in relation to EFA (Unterhalter 2014a).

The MDGs and EFA goals have been influential in providing a policy and advocacy framework as a means of attracting and channelling development assistance, and in shaping a particular range of desired outcomes. Up to about 2010 they had considerable influence on the modalities of development interventions, although thereafter a number of themes, which were less straightforward to monitor and measure, such as learning outcomes, skills, gender equality, school-related gender-based violence (SRGBV), and higher education, began to attract considerable concern on a national and international level. Early childhood care, which was in the Dakar goals but not the MDGs, was seen as crucial for improving children's readiness for school, enhancing nutrition, and supporting women's education

With respect to EFA's six goals, the following summary can be provided with regard to progress:

EFA Goal 1 Early childhood care and education (ECCE): Globally, considerable progress has been made in achieving ECCE, but progress is uneven. Early childhood health is improving in some countries where measurement has been effected; child mortality and malnutrition rates have declined in many countries in all regions of the world. The

MDGs target for child mortality, on the other hand, is unlikely to be met. 2012 calculations indicate under five mortality at 48 deaths per 1,000 live births, equivalent to 6.6 million deaths, while in Africa and South Asia 25 per cent of children were short for their age (i.e. suffering from stunting), indicating a lack of essential nutrients in the early years (UNESCO 2014: 45), and causing irreversible damage to development potential among such children. Enrolment in preschool programmes has expanded over the past decade, but there is a wide range of providers, many of them in the private and informal sector, and there is concern at difficulties in delivering care that focuses on early childhood education and not just minimal supervision. Only 68 out of 141 countries with available data will have more than 80 per cent of pre-school-aged children in ECCE programmes in 2015 (UNESCO 2014: 45).

EFA Goal 2 Universal primary education: On current trends, the target for universal primary education will be missed; although the number of out-of-school children of primary school age was reduced from 108 million in 1999 to 57 million in 2011, 54 per cent of whom are girls (UNESCO 2014: 52). Half of the children out of school live in conflict-affected countries. There has been a significant expansion of enrolment in sub-Saharan Africa, but in 2011 22 per cent of children from this region were out of school, and only 50 per cent completed the full primary cycle. The rate of reduction was rapid between 1999 and 2004, but then started slowing, and progress has stalled since 2008. It is estimated that in 2015, only 68 out of 122 countries will achieve UPE, and in 15 countries less than 80 per cent of children in the age range from primary school will be enrolled (UNESCO 2014: 52).

EFA Goal 3 Youth and adult skills: Participation in lower secondary school increased from 72 per cent to 82 per cent of children in that age range between 1999 and 2011, but in low-income countries only about a third of children complete this level, and for families in the lowest income quintile it is only 14 per cent (UNESCO 2014: 62). Inequalities in completing lower secondary school are associated with income, gender, and location.

EFA Goal 4 Improving adult literacy: The global adult illiteracy rate fell from 24 per cent in 1990 to 16 per cent in 2011. However in some countries, particularly in Africa and South and West Asia, the combination of limited programmes to address adult illiteracy and rising populations have meant that the numbers of adults who cannot read and write has grown. Women comprise 66 per cent of adult illiterates (UNESCO 2014: 70)

EFA Goal 5 Gender parity and equality in education: Gender parity (the ratio of girls to boys) is a much attenuated measure of gender equality, which entails issues associated with what is learned, how girls and boys are treated, and what happens after school. Some of the discussion about goals and targets focused on how better to measure gender equality in education (Unterhalter 2014a). In 2011, only 60 per cent of countries with data had achieved gender parity in primary enrolments. In 2015 it is projected that in 12 countries, there will be only nine girls enrolled in school for every 10 boys. At secondary education level only 38 per cent of countries with available data had achieved gender parity. Poverty, ethnicity, and rurality have considerable bearing on which girls and boys enrol and remain in school (UNESCO 2014: 76).

EFA Goal 6 The quality of education: UNESCO calculations indicated that universal primary completion will not be achieved for the poor in some countries for two generations, while attainment in literacy and numeracy was lowest for the most vulnerable (UNESCO 2014: 95–98). In many areas, the expansion of enrolments was not accompanied by the training of more teachers, and large classes with inadequate facilities were common. There was considerable interest in undertaking citizen-led or other national programmes of learning assessment to hold governments accountable for the quality of education. Analyses of the MDGs show a similar pattern. The MDGs Report of 2014 finds that the enrolment rate for primary-school-aged children rose from 83 per cent to 90 per cent between 2000 and 2012. Most of the gains were achieved by 2007, after which progress stagnated (United Nations 2014: 5). The numbers who could not read and write were high, at 781 million adults and 126 million youths, 60 per cent of whom are women (United Nations 2014: 16). Gender disparities are more prevalent at higher levels of education, and although many women work, family-friendly policies have not been developed, limiting the ways that home and school might complement each other.

The goals set by the MDGs are now seen by many to have been important but insufficient, in that they aimed for universality of only primary level education (the first five or six years of schooling) and for the achievement of literacy. For young adults, MDG 2 neglects post-primary school access, the quality of learning, adult literacy, and engagements with gender equality in education that go beyond parity. It says nothing about secondary and tertiary level education, although expansion of access and improvement of quality in these sectors are crucial both to generate the teachers to expand the education system and to deliver on all the other MDGs.

In debates about what focus should be given to EFA beyond 2015 and to the place of education in the SDGs, a number of key themes emerged, namely:

Access: Achieving UPE, with renewed emphasis on learning outcomes and teaching about a number of key themes, including global citizenship and sustainability. Access to secondary and post-secondary education became major concerns.

Equity and equality: This became a major thread in the discussion with concern regarding defining this in terms of features of social exclusion
associated with gender, socio-economic status, ethnicity, and location, focusing on strategies for measurement, and posing a range of
ethical questions regarding what issues a focus on equalities raised
(McCowan & Unterhalter 2015).

Quality: Extensive discussion took place on how to define education quality
(Alexander 2014; Tikly & Barrett 2013), and what this would mean if
quality came to be included in the SDGs and post-2015 EFA. There were
differences in view as to whether quality entailed inputs, such as numbers of trained teachers or textbooks, or whether it was associated with
outputs, such as numbers of children attaining a particular level of learning. Some stressed that quality was a feature of learning and teaching
relationships and processes (Alexander 2014), and others linked it with
cultivating particular dispositions associated with social justice (Tikly
2011). Despite these contestations, a number of policy analysts stressed
the importance of equipping education systems to deliver education efficiently in order to secure goal attainment (Barber and Mourshed 2007).

Sustainable development goals

2015 was both the date for the review of the Dakar goals on EFA and achievement of the MDGs. Thus intense debate was generated in the education and
international development community on the experience with these frameworks and what should replace them (for examples see Mundy & Manion 2015;
Post2015.org: what comes after the MDGs?; Sayed et al. 2013; Sayed & Rashid
2014; Unterhalter 2014a; Unterhalter 2014b). After an initial period when it
seemed that the SDGs education goal and the post-2015 EFA framework might
look very different, there is now considerable alignment. The Muscat Agreement of 2014 (EFA 2014), reached after a series of meetings of member states
and interested NGOs convened by UNESCO, sets outs seven targets for EFA
under an overarching goal (Ensure equitable and inclusive quality education
and lifelong learning for all by 2030). This goal is linked with seven new global
education targets:

Target 1: By 2030, at least x%[5] of girls and boys are ready for primary school
through participation in quality early childhood care and educa-
tion, including at least one year of free and compulsory pre-primary
education, with particular attention to gender equality and the most
marginalised.

---

[5]   The targets for the education goal are still under discussion and have not yet been set.

Target 2: By 2030, all girls and boys complete free and compulsory quality basic education of at least 9 years and achieve relevant learning outcomes, with particular attention to gender equality and the most marginalised.

Target 3: By 2030, all youth and at least x% of adults reach a proficiency level in literacy and numeracy sufficient to fully participate in society, with particular attention to girls and women and the most marginalised.

Target 4: By 2030, at least x% of youth and y% of adults have the knowledge and skills for decent work and life through technical and vocational, upper secondary and tertiary education and training, with particular attention to gender equality and the most marginalised.

Target 5: By 2030, all learners acquire knowledge, skills, values and attitudes to establish sustainable and peaceful societies, including through global citizenship education and education for sustainable development.

Target 6: By 2030, all governments ensure that all learners are taught by qualified, professionally-trained, motivated and well-supported teachers.

Target 7: By 2030, all countries allocate at least 4–6% of their Gross Domestic Product (GDP) or at least 15–20% of their public expenditure to education, prioritising groups most in need; and strengthen financial cooperation for education, prioritising countries most in need.

It can be seen that these targets correspond to education phases (pre-primary, primary, and basic), but that UPE has now been extended so that the vision is that all children complete nine years of good-quality, basic education. There is now an explicit target with regard to upper secondary and tertiary level education, and vocational education is mentioned. While EFA does not address the content of education, the Muscat Agreement mentions, under Target 5, learning for global citizenship and sustainable development. The Dakar Framework on EFA did not mention teachers, while the Muscat Agreement has an explicit target relating to training teachers. It also requires countries to spend a set proportion of GDP and public expenditure on education, prioritising the marginalised.

The recommendations in *the Open Working Group proposal for Sustainable Development Goals* (2014) were very similar, although the draft had also included targets around disability and education facilities. In the first four sub-goals of the education goal for the SDGs (Goal 4), the main articulation of gender is 'eliminate gender disparities in education', thus focusing on (dis)parity rather than equality. In the other education goals gender is spoken of in terms of access, completion, learning outcomes, literacy, and numeracy. Gender equality is also highlighted as one of the areas of knowledge to be promoted in relation to sustainable development. There is also a concern with gender-equitable learning environments. These two threads go beyond the Muscat Agreement, which has dropped the gender goal in the Dakar Framework and is treating gender largely as a matter of counting numbers of girls and boys participating at different levels. One of the issues feminist commentators have raised is whether the lack of attention to gender issues in the education goal provides the knowledge and understanding to address gender inequalities and violence, as outlined in the proposed gender goal.

What is the current debate about future goal setting?

The education goal recommended by the Open Working Group looks very similar to that outlined at Muscat. The goal is to 'Ensure inclusive and equitable quality education and promote lifelong learning opportunities for all'. A broader objective must be to ensure coherence and exploit synergies with other development goals. It is clear that through expanding lifelong learning opportunities for all, education also has the potential to contribute to other SDGs; the SDGs concerned with poverty and economic development are but one example.

Social and economic development in poor regions and countries is closely associated with the concept of 'sustainable livelihoods', which are the capabilities, assets, and activities required for a means of living. The education and development literatures have not been well integrated in this livelihoods context. From an economic perspective, formal education can partly be conceived as a form of capital-building, which can prepare individuals and communities to engage effectively with challenges beyond the classroom. Thus a life-skills approach to formal education is a condition for personal development, responsible citizenship, productive livelihoods, and sustainable economic development (Poole et al. 2013).

An example of this is Mexico, where education has long been considered critical for economic development, and past policies and investment in education have addressed the limited concepts of enrolment and attendance, failing to meet issues of progression, quality, and relevance, even by Latin American standards (Santibañez, Vernez & Razquin 2005). There are stark regional disparities in terms of education, infrastructure, and poverty, with indigenous groups worse off in terms of illiteracy levels, gender equity, and basic infrastructure.

Mexico's conditional cash transfer programme is part of the social development strategy called *Progresa*, begun in 1997 and renamed *Oportunidades* in 2002. Among other things, it offers financial grants for children and young people up to the age of 22 to participate in formal education between the third grade of primary school and the third grade of secondary school. By 2005 the programme covered 24 per cent of the population, including practically all the households living in extreme poverty, most of whom are rural (Levy 2006). Nevertheless, access does not equate to quality: *Oportunidades* does not address the need for improving the quality of education, student progression, or the educational performance of the system as a whole. Developing and emerging economies and regions should prioritise effective and efficient rural education, which incorporates practical and technical skills appropriate to the rural context, and which will prepare young people to participate in the development of rural areas. The demand for viable rural economies will persist, with increasing opportunities for developing dynamic, innovative, and modern businesses within a profitable agricultural base. Educational policies must be tailored with targeted programmes of support, 're-skilling' young people to overcome the barriers to local development and enabling the exploitation of new opportunities (Poole et al. 2013).

New information and communication technologies (ICTs) create new opportunities for learning for disadvantaged peoples that are much more flexible. Consistent with the argument that EFA at primary level is affordable, resources need to be reallocated in order to address local objectives, with specific budgetary attention given to the hard-to-reach, especially in terms of learning technology. New ICT has the potential to formulate a superior pedagogy, allowing interactivity that is now the standard for communication. This needs well-educated teachers, with formal training designed specifically for the particularities of specific systems, like tele-education. There is also an important role for teachers in facilitating learning in addition to direct teaching. In the case of ethnic and linguistic minorities, the cultural and language situation is usually problematic: clear communication between students and teachers is important, requiring language skills for teachers appropriate to the communities among which they work. Decentralisation of education policy can sometimes address some of these issues, leading to new pedagogical models and language skills, improved teacher training, and classroom performance.

In a development context, formal education will interact strongly with issues such food security and health, and rural economic development opportunities pose challenges for standards of formal education. This is particularly the case in Africa where the education components of the SDGs need to facilitate not just formal participation in schooling, but engagement with the process of sustainability in its widest sense. Karembu has written with regard to food production in Africa:

'Agriculturalists agree that the long-term sustainability of existing food production systems will largely depend on appropriate uptake and application of modern science and technologies. Education, empowerment and motivation of young people to take up agricultural activities are a prerequisite for improved and sustainable food production in Africa given their big numbers. However, this is not an overnight endeavour and calls for long-term investment and an overhaul of agricultural education curricula and support systems that enable the youth to apply agricultural innovations in a pleasurable and profitable way. The mass media have an important role in changing this perception. With better opportunities for access to technologies, entrepreneurial skills and social marketing, young people could funnel their youthful idealism, energy and determination into a positive force for change within the agricultural sector.

This would ultimately result in sustainable production of the food required to support the growing population in Africa' (Karembu 2013: 97).

Similar themes and visions in other SDGs make particular demands of the education goals that still appear too narrowly focussed to provide this range of learning. This need for a broader integration of education and other development goals is explored further in the last chapter of this book.

References

Alexander, R. (2014 February). *Teaching and learning: The quality imperative revisited*. Keynote address at Conference of the Norwegian National Commission for UNESCO, Norad, the Norwegian Refugee Council and the University of Oslo, Oslo, Norway. Retrieved from http://www.robinalexander. org.uk/wp-content/uploads/2014/02/Alexander-Oslo-GMR-2014B.pdf

Barber, M. & Mourshed, M., (2007) How the World's Best Education Systems Come Out on Top, London & New York: McKinsey. Retrieved from http:// mckinseyonsociety.com/downloads/reports/Education/Worlds_School_ Systems_Final.pdf

Education for All (EFA). (2000) The Dakar Framework for Action - Education for All: Meeting Our Collective Commitments. Paris: UNESCO Retrieved from http://www2.unesco.org/wef/en-conf/dakframeng.shtm

Education for All (EFA). (2014). Muscat Agreement Post 2015 EFA goals and targets. Paris: United Nations Educational, Scientific and Cultural Organization. Retrieved from https://efareport.wordpress.com/2014/06/04/ the-muscat-agreement-new-proposed-post-2015-global-education-goal-and-targets-announced-today/

Karembu, M. (2013). Preparing youth for high-tech agriculture. In: R. B. Heap and D. J. Bennett (Eds.), *Insights: Africa's future... can biosciences contribute?* 91–97. Cambridge: Banson Publishers.

Levy, S. (2006). Progress against poverty: sustaining Mexico's Progresa-Oportunidades Program. Washington DC: Brookings Institution Press.

McCowan, T., & Unterhalter, E. (2015). Education and international development: practice, policy and research. London: Bloomsbury.

Mundy, K., & Manion, C. (2015). The Education for All initiative: history and prospects post-2015. In: T. McCowan & E. Unterhalter (Eds.), *Education and international development: practice, policy and research* 49-68. London: Bloomsbury.

Open Working Group of the General Assembly on Sustainable Development Goals. (2014) Open Working Group proposal for Sustainable Development Goals document A/68/970. New York: United Nations. Retrieved from http://undocs.org/A/68/970

Poole, N. D., Alvarez, F., Vazquez, R., & Penagos, N. (2013). Education for All and for what? Life-skills and livelihoods in rural communities. *Journal of Agribusiness in Developing and Emerging Economies, 3*(1), 64–78.

Post-2015.org: what comes after the MDGs? Retrieved from www http://post2015.org/

Santibañez, L., Vernez, G., & Razquin, P. (2005). Education in Mexico: challenges and opportunities. Santa Monica, CA: RAND Corporation.

Sayed, Y., & Rashid A. (2014). Education quality, and teaching and learning in the post-2015 education agenda. *International Journal of Educational Development, 40,* 330–338.

Sayed, Y., Sprague, T., UNESCO, UNICEF, Turner, D., Smith, A., Paulson, J., et al (2013). Post-2015 education and development – contestation, contradictions and consensus. Compare forum special issue on post-2015 education and development agenda. *Compare, 43*(6). DOI: http://dx.doi.org/10.1080/03057925.2013.850285

Tikly, L. (2011). Towards a framework for researching the quality of education in low-income countries, *Comparative Education, 47*(1), 1–23.

Tikly, L & Barrett, A (2013), 'Education quality and social justice in the South: Towards a conceptual framework'. in: L Tikly, A Barrett (eds) *Education Quality and Social Justice in the South: Challenges for policy, practice and research*. Routledge, 11-24

United Nations. (2014). The Millennium Development Goals Report 2014. New York: United Nations.

United Nations Educational, Scientific and Cultural Organization (UNESCO). (2014). Teaching and learning: achieving quality education for all. Paris: UNESCO.

Unterhalter, E. (2014a). Measuring education for the Millennium Development Goals: reflections on targets, indicators, and a post-2015 framework. *Journal of Human Development and Capabilities, 15*(1–2), 176–187.

Unterhalter, E. (2014b). Walking backwards to the future: a comparative perspective on education and a post-2015 framework. *Compare, 44*(6), 852–873

Governance and institutions[6]

Niheer Dasandi[*], David Hudson[*] and Tom Pegram[*]

*University College London, School of Public Policy,
Department of Political Science

Introduction

Governance, at both the global and national levels, has long been an important focus of international development efforts. However, while there is a long history of global goal setting, there has been very little goal setting on national governance and institutions. Global governance was incorporated into the MDGs as Goal 8 (Develop a global partnership for development), but there was no domestic governance goal. The proposed inclusion of Goal 16 in the SDGs (Promote peaceful and inclusive societies for sustainable development, provide access to justice for all and build effective, accountable and inclusive institutions at all levels) by the Open Working Group for Sustainable Development Goals (2014) is therefore genuinely novel and important. In this chapter we take a step back to try and clear up some conceptual confusion around the status of governance in international goal setting, as well as flag up the likely political challenges facing the SDGs. We evaluate the historical process of governance goal setting, progress in the area, and finally assess the current debates and propose the most important issues facing the future of governance and development goals.

Our starting point is a general definition of governance as 'the institutions, mechanisms or processes backed by political power and/or authority that allow an activity or set of activities to be controlled, influenced or directed in the collective interest' (Baker, Hudson & Woodward 2005: 4). This definition includes

---

[6] N. Dasandi, D. Hudson, and T. Pegram contributed equally to this work.

How to cite this book chapter:
Dasandi, N, Hudson, D, and Pegram, T. 2015. Governance and institutions. In:
Waage, J and Yap, C. (eds.) *Thinking Beyond Sectors for Sustainable Development.*
Pp. 63–76. London: Ubiquity Press. DOI: http://dx.doi.org/10.5334/bao.h

laws (hard and soft), regulations, and agreements; organisations (national, local and regional governments, international bodies, secretariats, NGOs, and businesses); shared norms of behaviour; and the balance of power therein. This definition allows us to make three key framing points that inform the rest of the chapter: domestic-global, goal-process, and management-politics.

First, a key distinction is the different, and often separate, debates around domestic and global governance. Second, it is important to be clear as to whether we are, and indeed should be referring to a governance goal, such as improving state capacity by x% or transparency by y%, or governance as the process by which other goals are achieved or delivered. Third, governance is often reduced to management; however, governance is really about politics, which is the collective social activity through which people make, preserve, and amend the rules that regulate the production, distribution, and use of resources (Heywood 2014; Lasswell 1936; Leftwich 2004). This means that governance is about much more than technical management, it is also fundamentally about power, interests, values, authority, and legitimacy. Governance not only concerns the distribution of power and wealth, but it is also the process through which the current system is maintained or contested.

What is the historical process by which goal setting in this sector has developed?

Since the emergence of international development as an area of global policy following the Second World War, there has been much emphasis placed on governance at the global and national levels. At the global level, the emphasis has traditionally been on the transfer of finance and knowledge from richer to poorer nations, while the focus on national governance centred around the belief that democracy was fundamental to the development process (Hudson and Dasandi 2014).

The United Nations Millennium Declaration, from which the MDGs evolved, makes explicit reference to promoting democracy and strengthening the rule of law (UNGA 2000). The MDGs partnership between richer and poorer nations is based on a 'compact', in which richer nations commit themselves to meeting aid obligations, while poorer countries provide the 'appropriate policy context for development', including good governance, sound economic decision making, transparency, accountability, rule of law, respect for human rights and civil liberties, and local participation (Greig et al. 2007; UNDP 2003). The question that arises, then, is why the MDGs themselves prioritised (an admittedly weak and non-binding) global governance goal while domestic governance goals were completely absent? We suggest three reasons.

First, United Nations member states (the donors in particular) were unable to agree on what a domestic governance goal should consist of (White and Black 2004). In particular, this relates to democracy. While this has been a normative principle of the donor countries, there has been a long debate on whether or not democracy is necessary for development, especially as a number of the most successful developing countries, particularly the East Asian 'tiger' economies, and now Rwanda and Ethiopia, have been autocratic. This doubt, plus collective concerns about sovereignty, helped trump any attempts to include a democracy goal.

Second, the MDGs were an explicit attempt to move away from the Washington Consensus and its associated aid conditionality where, to receive aid, and in particular emergency loans, developing countries had to implement a series of market-based policy reforms. The consensus was that this had been a failure (Chang 2003; Easterly 2001). Given this, there was a concerted effort to move from macroeconomic policy reform towards a results-based approach to human development goals (Greig et al. 2007; Wilkinson and Hulme 2012).

Third, the MDGs were based on an understanding of poverty promoted by Jeffrey Sachs, the director of the Millennium Project. For Sachs, poverty is a function of past poverty and adverse geography, not primarily bad governance (Sachs 2005; Sachs et al. 2004; UNDP 2006). As such, the MDGs framework was based on the premise that developing countries required a large amount of aid to escape their 'poverty trap' (Hudson 2015).

Hence, to move past macroeconomic aid conditionality, the international community moved away from emphasising domestic causes of poverty and instead focused on the global partnership. Yet since then, there has been growing attention given to the role of domestic political institutions as a primary obstacle to development. As such, there has been a shift away from focusing on global governance towards a greater focus on national governance.

What progress has been achieved in this sector through the Millennium Development Goals and other processes?

The MDGs had a limited focus on governance and institutions. Primarily, governance was conceived as the management of global cooperation and as the partnership between donors and partner countries. Yet MDG 8 was notable for its lack of quantified and time-bound targets (e.g. Target 8.A, Develop further an open, rule-based, predictable, non-discriminatory trading and financial system). It was characterised by somewhat oblique measures of a global partnership (e.g. Target 8.F, In cooperation with the private sector, make available the benefits of new technologies, especially information and communications). The goal's targets refer to donor aid commitments, duty-free imports, debt levels, and access to affordable drugs and internet penetration. But, as Clarke (2004) argues, the notion of 'partnership' in development has typically referred to aid. And this is a longstanding view, with donor aid targets dating as far back as the Pearson Commission (Hudson 2015; Pearson 1969).

Progress to date, as measured against the official MDG 8 indicators, has been mixed and moderate. Aid (Target 8.A), after falling in recent years, has picked up again in 2013 to hit a record high of US$134.8 billion (UNDP 2014). Since 1990, aid has increased by 56 per cent in absolute terms (at constant prices) (OECD 2014). However, in relative terms (as a proportion of donor budgets) it has fallen to from 0.32 per cent in 1990 to 0.3 per cent in 2013. Meanwhile non-DAC (Development Assistance Committee) donors are increasing their budgets, for example the United Arab Emirates gave 1.25 per cent of their national income in aid. Also importantly, less aid is going to the poorest countries and more is going to middle-income countries. While this reflects the changing geography of poverty (Sumner 2010), it adversely impacts on Targets 8.B and 8.C, which are to address the special needs of the least developed, landlocked developing countries and small-island developing States.

Duty-free market access has improved for developing countries, as the proportion of developed country imports has increased from 54 per cent in 1996 to 80 per cent of their exports in 2012 (UNDP 2014). However, market protection, especially by Japan, the US, and the EU, continues to protect clothing textiles and agricultural products (all key exports for many developing countries), so the question of precisely which goods and services lie within this 20 per cent matters a great deal. Furthermore, the advantage that the LDCs have had over other developing countries is being steadily eroded as average tariff levels have fallen.

Debt levels have fallen in recent years (Target 8.D), with the average debt burden of developing countries standing at 3.1 per cent in 2012 (as a proportion of foreign debt service to exports revenue); it was 12 per cent in 2000. However, seasoned observers are flagging up a large increase of 75% in foreign loans to low-income countries, and a doubling of loans to sub-Saharan African countries between 2008 and 2012 (Jones 2014). The increasingly widespread use of mobile-cellular and information technologies has been well documented. The latest figures report that, by the end of 2014, 40 per cent of the world will be using the internet and there will be seven billion mobile phone subscriptions (with many people holding multiple accounts) (UNDP 2014).

Beyond the MDGs, other processes have fed into or can be used to track progress on governance. The Paris Declaration on Aid Effectiveness in 2005 and the resulting Accra Agenda for Action (OECD 2008) identified a set of principles to improve the quality of donor aid by strengthening, harmonising, and aligning developing country governance structures and processes with international aid systems. Similar to the MDGs, the Declaration was built around a set of indicators and targets that were to be met by 2010 (OECD 2008). The 2011 final report on progress was a 'sobering' read (OECD 2011): only one of the 13 targets had been met by 2010.

Finally, the Worldwide Governance Indicators (WGIs) are used by the World Bank to track six dimensions of governance (Kaufmann, Kraay & Mastruzzi 2010). They cover the following dimensions: Voice and Accountability, Political Stability and Absence of Violence, Government Effectiveness, Regulatory Quality, Rule of Law, and Control of Corruption. The time series data shows a relatively static picture since 1996, with the global averages showing no clear pattern of systematic improvements or declines (Kaufmann, Kraay & Mastruzzi 2010). However, the authors note that at an individual country level, over one time period such as a decade, around eight per cent of countries will typically show a significant improvement or decline.

Meanwhile, in academic debates, there has been huge progress in understanding the role of domestic political institutions in development. While the original work was spearheaded by Douglass North (1991), the most influential work has been Daron Acemoglu, Simon Johnson, and James Robinson (2001, 2002) whose use of historic data and new econometric techniques enabled them to make strong causal claims about the role of institutions in development. It is worth noting that these causal claims were made by directly comparing the impact of political institutions with Sachs' claims about geography. The findings led to something of a consensus among prominent development researchers that 'institutions rule' (Rodrik, Subramanian & Trebbi 2004). It is this new perspective that has led to the inclusion of a national governance goal in the proposed goals put forward by the High-Level Panel of Eminent Persons on the Post-2015 Development Agenda.

What is the current debate about future goal setting?

As noted, the major debate around the SDGs with respect to governance is whether and how to include a domestic governance goal (e.g. Bates-Eamer et al. 2012; Foresti & Wild 2014; Transparency International 2010, 2013). Specific governance targets being proposed include rule of law, budget and procurement integrity and transparency, citizen engagement, corruption and bribery, service delivery effectiveness, civil liberties, freedom of the press, access to justice, gender rights, property rights, breadth of the tax base, and so forth. The more interesting aspect of this debate is whether to have a stand-alone set of governance targets versus governance targets within each goal; for example a governance target for maternal health, a governance target for the environment, and so forth. Or, as Marta Foresti (2014:1) has persuasively argued, 'focusing all efforts on a 'stand-alone' goal risks missing the point. All eggs are being placed in one basket rather than in a wider strategy to put governance on the global agenda for the next 15 years.' Our argument builds on this and suggests that the real issues around governance and sustainable development lie 'above' and 'below' the level of national institutions.

Coordinating action across multiple SDGs raises very serious challenges in terms of regime fragmentation, as well as the particular problem structures and strategic environments distinct issue areas reveal. For example, the prospects for strengthening the implementation of the World Health Organization Framework Convention on Tobacco Control (proposed Goal 3.a) presents a very different problem structure in terms of existing cross-sectoral capabilities and interest-alignment and implementation mechanisms, compared to halving global food waste and reducing food losses along production and supply chains (proposed Goal 12.3). Other SDGs, such as assisting developing countries in attaining long-term debt sustainability (proposed Goal 17.4), may conflict with the financial rules of international financial institutions like the International Monetary Foundation (Open Working Group of the General Assembly on Sustainable Development Goals 2014).

There is a double risk: on the one hand retreat into silo particularisms and policy prescriptions which do not account for the cross-cutting nature of many of the goals or, equally problematic, an overambitious governance frame which identifies all of these issues as facets of the same problem, but offers little in the way of concrete solutions. The solution is not just to look for win-wins, but to cluster linked SDGs whose solution is likely to hinge on understanding and ameliorating negative interactions (for instance, assuring all people have access to adequate, affordable, safe and nutritious food and phasing out all forms of agricultural support subsidies).

First, 'below'. It is now increasingly accepted that politics is central to explaining development outcomes (Carothers and de Gramont 2013; DFID 2010; Leftwich 2000, 2005; Wild & Foresti 2011). Effectively and successfully governing and managing the interactions between different sectors and development goals is always inherently a political question. It is always possible to identify governance gaps and to design suitable and necessary institutional arrangements to fill these gaps. However, the subsequent questions of whether or not these institutions are put in place, receive the necessary resources and support to operate, and can effectively implement their objectives boils down to the question of 'political will'. Anyone interested in the success of the goals will need to engage in some serious political analysis (Fritz et al. 2014; Hudson and Leftwich 2014; IDS 2010; Unsworth & Williams 2011; UNDP 2012; Wild & Foresti 2011).

Second, 'above'. Effective implementation clearly depends upon domestic configurations of institutions and political will. However, there is no getting away from the supra-national aspect of governance for sustainable development, given the irreducibly global nature of the challenge. Many developmental issues, from forest stewardship, to soil fertility, desertification, and air pollution, can only be addressed at the global level, given their transboundary character. In addition, issues conventionally perceived as domestic (read sovereign), such as poverty eradication, non-communicable disease control, health system reform, and educational provision, may also have a crucial global dimension. This is especially true as the policy space for delivering public goods is increasingly circumscribed by prescriptive economic models and expansive transnational trade regulation.

The sustainable development agenda demands coordinated action at the global level. Institutions are required to limit the negative externalities of decentralised action, to provide focal points for coordinated action, to deal with systemic disruptions in a global context of growing interdependence and complexity, and provide some form of safeguard against severe deprivation and hardship (Keohane 2001). Sustainability and development deal with issues that do not conform to established political boundaries and require management and steering at multiple levels of authority. Scholars and practitioners have acknowledged the challenge of approaching questions of global governance in a coherent fashion (Thakur 2009). Further, in a context where power is distributed across diverse societal subsystems and among many societal actors the challenge of managing transformative change is increased (Meadowcroft 2014: 300). We illustrate these issues through a discussion of the governance of sustainable development, as well as drawing out lessons on the importance of institutional stewardship in a context of complex and competing goals (such as we have with the SDGs).

Global governance of sustainable development has a long history of goal setting, initiated with the United Nations Conference on the Human Environment held in Stockholm in 1972 and the establishment of the UNEP. However, it is the United Nations Conference on Environment and Development (UNCED) held in Rio de Janeiro in 1992 that defined the global agenda. The UNCED established the Commission on Sustainable Development (CSD), a United Nations entity mandated to monitor and review progress on globally agreed goals and targets. The Rio Declaration on Environment and Development provides an exhaustive 'blueprint' for implementation of sustainable development, containing 27 principles on development and the environment. Alongside this, the 300-page Agenda 21 document sets out international and national objectives, and provides programmatic suggestions on how to fulfil those objectives, with more than 1,000 specific policy recommendations across four principal domains: social and economic dimensions, conservation and management of resources for development, strengthening the role of major groups, and means of implementation (UNEP Agenda 21).[7] The UNCED also produced a series of important global governance mechanisms including new multilateral environmental conventions (the UNFCCC).

Nevertheless, the Rio Conventions inaugurated what has been described as a 'golden age' in international norm-setting (Pattberg &Widerberg 2015, in press). The 1990s saw a series of significant advances in sustainable development regulatory frameworks, including the creation of the United Nations Intergovernmental Panel on Forests, the Kyoto Protocol, the Global Programme of Action for the Protection of the Marine Environment from Land-based Activities, and the United Nations guidelines on sustainable consumption. However, observers have noted that since 2000, there has appeared to be a 'stagnation' in international law (Pauwelyn, Wessel & Wouters 2012). On the other hand, we have witnessed the rapid growth of specialised and relatively autonomous

---

[7] Agenda 21 has been reaffirmed and modified at subsequent United Nations meetings.

rule or rule-complexes, often driven by private institutions and transnational networks.

The impact of global frameworks on sustainable development has been underwhelming, with Agenda 21 criticised as having 'failed to serve as a useful guide to action' (Thakur 2009). Since 2003, the CSD has served as the United Nations' hub for coordination on sustainable development, but is widely regarded as ineffective, buried in delegation chains of bureaucracy within the United Nations, and lacking implementation prerogatives or a financing mechanism (Cruickshank, Schneeberger & Smith 2012). For many observers, the global machinery underpinning a sustainable development agenda is not fit for purpose. Global structures and enhancing interagency coordination has been on the agenda since the World Summit on Sustainable Development (WSSD) in Johannesburg in 2002. Against a backdrop of accelerating unsustainable development, reform in global structures has struggled to keep pace (IPCC 2013).

In terms of institutional stewardship, Agenda 21 asserted the role of UNEP as the leading global environmental authority and produced a series of recommendations in order to strengthen its governance function. This was duly recognised by the United Nations General Assembly in December 2012. However, concerns persist over the goodness of fit of the UNEP mandate and sustainable development, which includes environment, but also goes beyond to engage issues of resource management and social and economic dimensions. **Figure 1** provides some initial insight into the sustainable development regime complex within the United Nations system. There is no coordinating mechanism within the system dedicated to managing the sustainable development complex. This governance arrangement has exacerbated difficulties in prioritisation of sustainable development objectives, leading to a silo as opposed to an integrated approach towards the three core pillars of Agenda 21: economic, social, and environmental. Post-Rio+20, UNEP has been elevated to the status of a United Nations programme. However, its jurisdiction is principally confined to environmental protection, has no authority to enforce environmental regulation, and suffers from chronic underfunding. The 2012 reform elevated UNEP's relationship with the General Assembly, however, it remains a subsidiary programme as opposed to a more robust and autonomous specialised agency such as the WHO. Although a proposal to upgrade UNEP to a specialised agency was tabled at Rio+20, as well as the possibility of superseding it with a United Nations environmental organisation, neither idea prospered. The natural coordinating mechanism within the system of the United Nations might be the CSD. However, its impact is widely regarded as underwhelming: it suffers from low-grade status as a functional commission to the United Nations Economic and Social Council (ECOSOC), has no implementation or financing apparatus, and has little strategic impact on national or international policy making (Cruickshank, Schneeberger & Smith 2012).

Food & Agriculture Regime
- FAO*
- IFAD*
- WFP**

Health Regime
- WHO*
- UNAIDS**

Development Regime
- UNDP**
- World Bank Group
- Status of women***
- UN-HABITAT**
- UNICEF**
- UNIDO*
- CSD***

Sustainable Development Regime Complex

Trade regime
- WTO
- IMF*
- ITC
- WIPO*
- UNCTAD**

Human Rights Regime
- OHCHR
- Human Rights Council
- Treaties (ICCPR, ICESCR)

Climate regime
- UNEP**
- IMO*
- Forum on Forests***

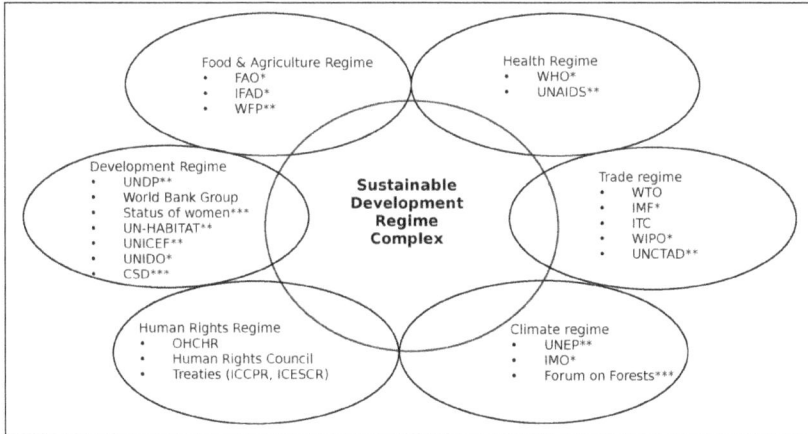

Figure 1: The Sustainable Development Regime Complex.

This figure is not exhaustive, but illustrates some of the main agencies and institutions in the global sustainable development regime complex where substantial rule-making efforts have occurred. This complex is focused on the United Nations human rights system, and does not include multilateral, bilateral, or private rule-making domains. * Specialised agency, ** GA/ECOSOC fund/programme, *** Functional commission.

Key: CSD: Commission on Sustainable Development; FAO: Food and Agriculture Organization; ICCPR: International Covenant on Civil and Political Rights; ICESCR: International Covenant on Economic, Social and Cultural Rights; IFAD: International Fund For Agricultural Development; IMF: International Monetary Fund; IMO: International Maritime Organization; ITC: International Trade Centre; OHCHR: Office of the High Commissioner for Human Rights; UNAIDS: Joint United Nations Programme on HIV/AIDS; UNCTAD: United Nations Conference on Trade and Development; UNDP: United Nations Development Programme; UNEP: United Nations Environmental Programme; UN-HABITAT: United Nations Human Settlements Programme; UNICEF: United Nations Children's Fund; UNIDO: United Nations Industrial Development Organization; WFP: World Food Programme; WHO: World Health Organization; WIPO: World Intellectual Property Organization; WTO: World Trade Organization.

So, given this, how best to design effective delivery of the SDGs? Much of the governance literature has sought to enhance the effectiveness of governance arrangements through effective management of participating states and other actors. Reliance on market mechanisms, materials incentives, and sanctions to reduce transaction costs and secure credible commitments remains a powerful influence on the governance debate today. Scholarship on multilevel governance emphasises efficiency gains through coordination, and functional and stratificatory differentiation across regimes (Zürn & Faude 2013). Put simply, a fragmented regime complex, as displayed in **Figure 1**, can be efficient where there is clear division of labour, specialisation, and role differentiation among institutions operating at different levels of governance (Biermann et al. 2009). However, the necessary condition for effective governance is effective regime management. Without regime cohesion and rule-system stewardship, the whole is unlikely to be greater than the sum of its parts. Indeed, we now understand all too well the obstacles to cooperation and enforcement when faced with asymmetric negative externalities (Mitchell & Keilbach 2001).

In turn, such governance frameworks privilege interests and underappreciate the role of power, values, and history in determining the preferences of member states when confronted with the benefits and trade-offs of cooperating on sustainable development. As observed in the collapse of global trade negotiations at the World Trade Organization (WTO), the usual mechanisms of interstate bargaining, such as reciprocity, have been no match for powerful historical grievances amid the rise of the G20 emerging economies (Young 2007). Pascal Lamy, the former Director-General of the WTO, has called for a new 'Geneva Consensus' in international trade negotiation: one which is sensitive to both global and local social, economic, and political contexts (Lamy 2013). Guided by the concept of subsidiarity (decisions should be made at as local a level as possible), others have employed a polycentric bottom-up governance approach (Abbott 2012).

To conclude, the SDGs agenda demands an evaluation of the acceptable bounds of natural, human, and human-produced capital if the biosphere and ecosystem is to be preserved. It is also an opportunity to urgently take stock of the governance actors and structures currently dedicated to the task of accelerating change at all levels of human activity, including perhaps the most important of the proposed SDGs: transformation of consumption and production patterns. A lot of faith continues to be placed in a market-based approach to sustainable development. However, it is incumbent upon sustainable development policy architects to acknowledge the fundamental limitations of the market to provide public goods. SDGs governance architecture is not simply a realm of harmonising interests in pursuit of coordination, it also requires a serious engagement with politics and power. The key factors here are political action by public authorities at all levels, the capacity to build broad-based and plural coalitions of support, and the deployment of a range of principled instruments, including legal instruments, to ensure sustainable development.

References

Abbott, K. W. (2012). The transnational regime complex for climate change. *Government and Policy*, *30*(4), 571–590.

Acemoglu, D., Johnson, S., & Robinson, J. A. (2001). The colonial origins of comparative development: an empirical investigation. *American Economic Review*, *91*(5), 1369–1401.

Acemoglu, D., Johnson, S., & Robinson, J. A. (2002). Reversal of fortune: geography and institutions in the making of the modern world income distribution. *The Quarterly Journal of Economics*, *117*(4), 1231–1294.

Baker, A., Hudson, D., & Woodward, R. (2005). Introduction. In: A. Baker, D. Hudson, & R. Woodward (Eds.), *Governing financial globalisation: international political economy and multi-level governance*. London: Routledge. 3–23.

Bates-Eamer, N., Carin, B., Lee, M.H., Lim, W. & Kapila, M. (2012). Post-2015 development agenda: goals, targets and indicators. Ontario: CIGI & KDI. Retrieved from http://www.cigionline.org/sites/default/files/MDG_Post_2015v3.pdf

Biermann, F. Pattberg, P. and van Asselt, H. (2009). The Fragmentation of Global Governance Architectures: A Framework for Analysis. *Global Environmental Politics*, 9(4), 14–40.

Biermann, F., Abbott, K., Andresen, S., Backstrand, K., Bernstein, S., Betsill, M. M., Bulkeley, H., et al. (2012). Navigating the anthropocene: improving earth system governance. *Science*, *335*, 1306–1307.

Black, R., & White, H. (Eds.) (2004). *Targeting development: critical perspectives on the Millennium Development Goals*. Basingstoke: Routledge.

Carothers,T. & de Gramont, D. (2013). *Development aid confronts politics: The almost revolution*. Washington, DC: Carnegie Endowment for International Peace.

Chang, H-J. (2003). The Market, the State and Institutions in Economic Development. In Chang, H-J. (Ed.) *Rethinking Development Economics*, London: Anthem Press. 41–60.

Clarke, P. (2004). Building a global partnership for development? In: Black, R., & White, H. (Eds.) *Targeting development: critical perspectives on the Millennium Development Goals*. Basingstoke: Routledge.

Cruickshank, E. W., Schneeberger, K., & Smith, N. (Eds.) (2012). A pocket guide to sustainable development governance 2nd Edition. London: Commonwealth Secretariat Stakeholder Forum. 12

Department for International Development (DfID) (2010). *The Politics of Poverty: Elites, Citizens and States. Findings from ten years of DFID-funded research on Governance and Fragile States 2001-2010*. London: DFID

Easterly, W. (2001). The Lost Decades: Developing Countries' Stagnation in Spite of Policy Reform 1980–1998. *Journal of Economic Growth*, 6 (2): 135–157

Fritz, V., Levy, B. & Ort, R. (2014). *Problem-Driven Political Economy Analysis: The World Bank's Experience*. Washington DC: World Bank. Retrieved from http://elibrary.worldbank.org/doi/book/10.1596/978-1-4648-0121-1

Foresti, M., Wild, L., Rodriguez Takeuchi, L., & Norton, A. (2014). *Governance targets and indicators for post 2015: An initial assessment*. London: Overseas Development Institute.

Greig, A., Hulme, D. and Turner, M. (2007) *Challenging Global Inequality: Development Theory and Practice in the 21st Century*. Basingstoke: Palgrave Macmillan.

Heywood, A. (2014). Politics, 4th Edition. Basingstoke: Palgrave.

Hudson, D. & Leftwich, A. (2014). From Political Economy to Political Analysis. *DLP Research Paper 25*, Retrieved from http://www.dlprog.org/publications/from-political-economy-to-political-analysis.php

Hudson, D. & Dasandi, N. (2014). The global governance of development: development financing, good governance and the domestication of poverty. In: A. Payne, N. Phillips (Eds.), *Handbook of the International Political Economy of Governance*. Cheltenham: Edward Elgar, 238–258.

Hudson, D. (2015). Global finance and development. Abingdon: Routledge.

Institute of Development Studies (IDS). (2010). An Upside Down View of Governance. Brighton: Institute of Development Studies. Retrieved from http://www2.ids.ac.uk/gdr/cfs/pdfs/AnUpside-downViewofGovernance.pdf

Intergovernmental Panel on Climate Change (IPCC). (2013): *Working group i contribution to the IPCC fifth assessment report climate change 2013: the physical science basis*. Retrieved from http://www.climatechange2013.org/images/uploads/WGIAR5_WGI-12Doc2b_FinalDraft_Chapter09.pdf

Jones, T. (2014). 'Don't turn the clock back': analysing the risks of the lending boom to impoverished countries. London: Jubilee Debt Campaign. Retrieved from http://jubileedebt.org.uk/wp-content/uploads/2014/10/Lending-boom-research_10.14.pdf

Kaufmann, D., Kraay, A., & Mastruzzi, M. (2010). The Worldwide Governance Indicators: methodology and analytical issues (World Bank Policy Research Working Paper No. 5430). Washington DC: World Bank. Retrieved from http://ssrn.com/abstract=1682130

Keohane, R. (2001). Governance in a partially globalised world. *American Political Science Review, 95*(1), 1–13.

Lamy, P. (2013). *The Geneva Consensus: making trade work for all*. Cambridge: Cambridge University Press.

Lasswell, H. (1936). *Politics: who gets what, when, how?* New York: McGraw-Hill.

Leftwich, A. (2000). *States of development: On the primacy of politics in development*. Cambridge: Polity.

Leftwich, A. (2005). Politics in Command: Development Studies and the Rediscovery of Social Science, *New Political Economy*, 10(4), 573–607.

Leftwich, A. (Ed.) (2004). *What is politics? The activity and its study*. Cambridge: Polity.

Meadowcroft, J. (2014). Who is in charge here? Governance for sustainable development in a complex world. *Journal of Environmental Policy & Planning*, 9(3–4), 299–314.

Mitchell, R. B., & Keilbach, P. M. (2001). Situation structure and institutional design: reciprocity, coercion, and exchange. *International Organisation*, 55(4), 891–917.

North, D. C. (1991). Institutions, institutional change and economic performance. Cambridge, Cambridge University Press.

Open Working Group of the General Assembly on Sustainable Development Goals. (2014) Open Working Group proposal for Sustainable Development Goals document A/68/970. New York: United Nations. Retrieved from http://undocs.org/A/68/970

Organisation for Economic Co-operation and Development (OECD). (2008). The Accra Agenda for Action. Paris: OECD. Retrieved from www.oecd.org/development/effectiveness/34428351.pdf

Organisation for Economic Co-operation and Development (OECD). (2011). Aid effectiveness 2005–10: progress in implementing the Paris Declaration. Paris: OECD. Retrieved from http://effectivecooperation.org/files/resources/2011%20Report%20on%20Monitoring%20the%20Paris%20Declaration%20ENGLISH.pdf

Organisation for Economic Co-operation and Development (OECD). (2014). OECD. Stat (database). Paris: OECD. Retrieved from http://dx.doi.org/10.1787/data-00285-en

Pattberg, P., & Widerberg, O. The global governance of the environment. *Millennium*, Spring 2015, (in press).

Pauwelyn, J., Wessel, R. A., & Wouters, J. (2012). Informal international lawmaking. Oxford: Oxford University Press.

Pearson, L. B. (1969). Partners in development: report of the Commission on International Development. London: Pall Mall Press.

Rodrik, D., Subramanian, A., & Trebbi, F. (2004). Institutions rule: the primacy of institutions over geography and integration in economic development. *Journal of Economic Growth*, 9(2), 131–165.

Sachs, J. (2005). *The End of Poverty.* London: Penguin.

Sachs, J.D., McArthur, J.W., Schmidt-Traub, G., Kruk, M., Bahadur, C., Faye M. and McCord G. (2004). Ending Africa's Poverty Trap. *Brookings Paper on Economic Activity*, 35 (1): 117–240.

Sumner, A. (2010). Global poverty and the new bottom billion: three-quarters of the world's poor live in middle-income countries. *IDS Working Papers, 2010*(349).

Thakur, R. (2009). The global governance of sustainable development. In: T. G. Weiss, & R. Thakur, *The United Nations and global governance.* Bloomington: Indiana University Press. 199-226.

Transparency International (2010) *The Anti-Corruption Catalyst: Realising the MDGs by 2015.* Berlin: Transparency International.

Transparency International (2013). 2015 and Beyond: The governance solution for development. *Transparency International Working Paper 01/2013.* Berlin: Transparency International.

United Nations Development Programme (UNDP). (2003) *Human Development Report 2003: Millennium Development Goals: A Compact among Nations to End Poverty.* Oxford: Oxford University Press.

United Nations Development Programme (UNDP). (2006) *Human Development Report 2006: Beyond Scarcity: Power, Poverty and the Global Water Crisis.* Basingstoke: Palgrave/United Nations Development Programme.

United Nations Development Programme (2012). *Institutional and Context Analysis.* New York: UNDP.

United Nations Development Programme (UNDP). (2014). The Millennium Development Goals Report 2014. New York: United Nations.

United Nations Environment Programme (UNEP). *Agenda 21.* Retrieved from http://www.unep.org/Documents.Multilingual/Default.asp?documentid=52

United Nations General Assembly (UNGA). (2000). United Nations Millennium Declaration, Resolution adopted by the General Assembly [without reference to a Main Committee (A/55/L.2)] 55/2. New York: United Nations.

Unsworth, S., & Williams, G. (2011). Political economy analysis to improve EU development effectiveness. DEVCO concept paper. Retrieved from http://www.delog.org/cms/upload/pdf-pea/Using_political%20Economy_Analsysis.pdf

Wild, L., & Foresti, M. (2011). Politics into practice. A dialogue on governance strategies and action in international development. London: Overseas Development Institute.

Wilkinson, R., & Hulme, D. (Eds.) (2012). *The Millennium Development Goals and beyond: global development after 2015.* Basingstoke: Routledge.

Young, A. (2007). Trade politics ain't what it used to be: the European Union in the Doha round. *Journal of Common Market Studies, 45*(4), 789–811.

Zürn, M., & Faude, B. (2013). On fragmentation, differentiation, and coordination. *Global Environmental Politics, 13*(3), 119–130.

PART II

Thinking Beyond Sectors

Governing Sustainable Development Goals: interactions, infrastructures, and institutions

Jeff Waage[*], Christopher Yap[†], Sarah Bell[‡],
Caren Levy[§], Georgina Mace[¶] Tom Pegram[**],
Elaine Unterhalter[††], Niheer Dasandi[**],
David Hudson[**], Richard Kock[‡‡],
Susannah H. Mayhew[§§], Colin Marx[§]
and Nigel Poole[¶¶]

[*]London International Development Centre; School of Oriental and African Studies, Centre for Development, Environment and Policy, [†]London International Development Centre; University College London, Bartlett Development Planning Unit, [‡]University College London, Centre for Environmental and Geomatic Engineering, [§]University College London, Bartlett Development Planning Unit, [¶]University College London, Centre for Biodiversity and Environment Research, [**]University College London, School of Public Policy, [††]University College London, Institute of Education, Department of Humanities and Social Sciences, [‡‡]Royal Veterinary College, Department of Pathology and Pathogen Biology, [§§]London School of Hygiene and Tropical Medicine, Department of Global Health and Development, [¶¶]School of Oriental and African Studies, Centre for Environment, Development and Policy

Introduction

Sustainable development is hard to define and harder to achieve. The process of expansion from eight MDGs with 18 targets and 48 indicators, to proposals

How to cite this book chapter:
Waage, J, Yap, C, Bell, S, Levy, C, Mace, G, Pegram, T, Unterhalter, E, Dasandi, N, Hudson, D, Kock, R, Mayhew, S. H, Marx, C, and Poole, N. 2015. Governing Sustainable Development Goals: interactions, infrastructures, and institutions. In: Waage, J and Yap, C. (eds.) *Thinking Beyond Sectors for Sustainable Development*. Pp. 79–88. London: Ubiquity Press. DOI: http://dx.doi.org/10.5334/bao.i

for 17 SDGs with over 100 indicators, demonstrates the evolving awareness by the international community of the complex nature of development and its implications for society, the economy, and the environment. Whilst the development of goals, targets, and indicators shows a stronger commitment to defining and monitoring constituent elements, sustainable development is more than the sum of its parts. It is an outcome of positive synergies between multiple elements, and may be undermined by negative trade-offs between them.

The proposed SDGs have been informed, influenced, and developed by different sectoral constituencies. As with the MDGs (Waage et al. 2010), this process has not sufficiently addressed the interactions between goals, and between the mechanisms and processes that could be established to achieve them. These interactions could be positive or negative, and the nature of them may be physical, physiological, socio-political, or any combination thereof. The challenge for achieving sustainable development is how to manage and govern these interactions.

The experience of the MDGs shows that strong institutional ownership of goals made them more likely to be delivered. However, while the MDGs were coherent on systems of measurement, they were weak in facilitating participation and voice in relation to reviewing implementation (Hulme 2013). Similar governance mechanisms for the newly proposed SDGs, such as those pertaining to the management of climate change and the environment, have so far proved difficult to establish.

Governance in terms of responsibility, transparency, accountability, capacity, and legitimacy at sub-national, national, and international levels is essential for achieving sustainable development. A successful governance process for the SDGs, which engages with the full range of political interests, would link the delivery of goals that are capable of synergy, and negotiate trade-offs to optimise delivery of goals that are in conflict; governance within silos is no longer tenable.

This chapter proposes a framework for classifying and clustering goals and their interactions, uses this to identify the different problem structures and challenges for governance, and proposes potential solutions. We use this novel conceptualisation to show why different goals interact positively or negatively, and where and why governing these interactions can lead to a 'win-win', as well as where governing these interactions is a much more politically difficult challenge.

Levels of sustainable development

The framework is based on the SDGs as proposed in the *Report of the Open Working Group of the General Assembly on Sustainable Development Goals* (2014). It consists of three levels, to which we assign goals based on their intended outcomes. This is illustrated in **Figure 2**.

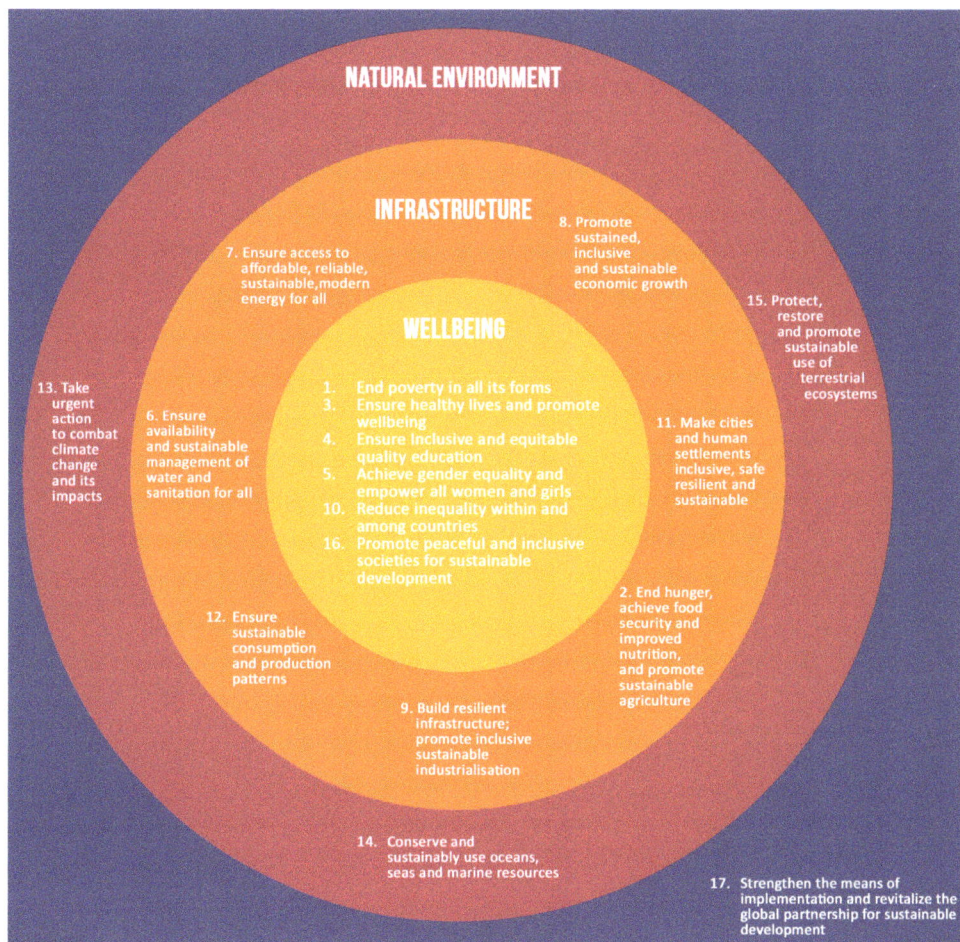

Figure 2: The SDGs as proposed in the *Report of the Open Working Group of the General Assembly on Sustainable Development Goals*, placed in the proposed framework.[8]

---

[8] The goals have been paraphrased in the above diagram, for the full list of proposed goals see the Appendix. The placement of goals in particular parts of this diagram is approximate. For a few goals, the proposed sub-goals and targets actually spread across different levels. For instance, the water-related targets of Goal 6 address environmental (water resource), infrastructural (useable capacity), and well-being (sanitation) levels, while the agriculture-related targets of Goal 2 address infrastructural (production) and well-being (hunger) levels. Please note that the concentric levels do not represent geographical scale in a narrow sense, but different ways in which the goals impact. All goals must have mechanisms for delivery on local, national, and global scales.

The inner level, *Well-Being*, includes 'people-centred' goals that aim to deliver individual and collective outcomes, such as health, education, and nutrition, which directly pertain to welfare and well-being and their equitable distribution within and between individuals and countries. They represent well-established terrain for governments and are a key component of accountability (the social contract between the state and society) and state legitimation strategies. The MDGs established some minimal lines of delivery for goals of this kind, but the draft SDGs represent a more ambitious attempt to support well-being and welfare in additional areas, such as promoting peaceful and inclusive societies, where governments have less experience.

The middle level, *Infrastructure*, includes goals that relate to various kinds of networks and mechanisms for the production, distribution, and delivery of goods and services, including food, energy, clean water, and waste and sanitation services in cities and human settlements. These goals transcend individuals, households, and communities, and address many of the perceived essential functions of modern society within and sometimes beyond nation states. They are assumed to contribute to growth in well-being while at the same time reducing intensity of resource use, pollution, and negative impacts on the environment.

The outer level, *Environment*, groups together those goals that relate primarily to the management of global resources, underlying support systems and global public goods such as land, ocean, air, natural resources, biodiversity, and the management of climate change. Here are the biophysical systems that underpin sustainable development. While not dependent on human activities, these systems are strongly influenced by them. These goals typically require international and transnational cooperation for their realisation.

We have left Goal 17, relating to revitalising the global partnership for sustainable development, outside our three levels because it is a cross-cutting goal relating to goals in all levels.

Interactions

This framework clarifies the major interactions between groups of goals. Optimally, all goals contribute to improving agreed measures of individual and community well-being (health, education, income, security, and so forth). However, the potential positive and negative interactions between all SDGs are closely associated with their positioning at different levels in our framework.

In general, interactions between goals in the inner level pose opportunities for positive synergies and win-wins, because of their similar relation to notions of human development, and focus on individual and community well-being. Examples include the synergies that could be achieved by aligning the design of health, gender, and education goals to improve sexual and reproductive health (SRH), as well as the empowerment of women and girls, or between nutrition and education goals to improve early years development. The particular example of SRH is developed further in the next chapter.

Interactions between the inner and middle levels are mutually supportive. The importance of achieving the goals in the middle level to the inner level is clear: improving access to water, food, energy, and so forth, are all necessary to achieve the inner level, people-centred outcomes. However, there is also significant reciprocal influence, such as the positive impact of an educated, healthy labour force on agricultural production. The interactions between the outer and middle levels characterise the ways in which human societies appropriate environmental resources and services. 'Sustainability', a component of several goals at the middle level, is linked to how these environmental services are used.

The complicated and poorly understood links between goals at the outermost and innermost levels mean that the objectives of infrastructural goals at the middle level are often unclear, easily contested, and subject to multiple demands which may be in conflict. For instance, achieving Goal 2 on sustainable agriculture and food security, which will contribute to improving well-being by reducing hunger, may require increased agricultural production with consequential adverse impacts on goals to tackle climate change (Goal 13) and protect marine (Goal 14) and terrestrial (Goal 15) ecosystems. Achieving Goal 7, relating to energy, or Goal 6, relating to wastewater treatment, with their benefits to education, health, and other well-being outcomes, may depend on increased energy generation that may also impact negatively on climate change and water resource management.

As a result, goals in the middle level must mediate potentially negative trade-offs between outer- and inner-level goals, and may interact negatively with each other as they compete for limited environmental resources, e.g. agriculture versus energy. The mechanisms that will need to be established to achieve the goals in the middle level must relate to goals in both the inner and outer levels, and arbitrate these interactions.

Outer-level goals relating to reducing climate change and safeguarding marine and terrestrial ecosystems, natural resources, and water supplies, are closely interrelated and there are potential positive synergies. For instance, improving forest conservation may reduce climate change, while tackling climate change may reduce the loss of coral reefs which are critical marine resources.

The challenges addressed by the outer-level goals relate largely to the challenges of sustainability imposed by goals in the middle level. More subtle and less direct, but still profound, is the influence of the inner level on the outer-level goals, such as the impact of increasing access to high-quality education and family planning services on reducing population growth, which otherwise increases demand for natural resources and the strain on the environment. The impact of population growth on the outer level is mitigated through mechanisms at the middle level.

The complexity of the interactions between goals located at different levels highlights the challenge of the SDGs as a global policy framework. At the global scale, there exists no structure, institution, or mechanism for governing these types of interactions, particularly where they involve conflicts. This creates substantial and important governance challenges for the SDGs.

Governance

Governance refers to the institutions, mechanisms, or processes backed by political power and/or authority that allow an activity or set of activities to be controlled, influenced, or directed in the collective interest (Baker et al. 2005). From this perspective, governance includes: the responsibility an actor has for controlling, influencing, or directing activities in the collective interest; being held accountable to the collective; and having the capacity, in terms of political power and resources, to direct activities towards the collective interest. Governance refers to, amongst others, hard and soft laws, regulations, agreements, institutions (national, local, and regional government; international bodies; secretariats; civil society; and the private sector), shared norms of behaviour, and the balance of power therein.

It has been proposed that the SDGs might have a single, overarching governance goal (United Nations High-Level Panel of Eminent Persons on the Post-2015 Development Agenda 2012), or alternatively, that each goal should have its own governance structure (Foresti 2014). However, our framework shares more parallels with the notion of polycentric governance, whereby multiple centres of authority with circumscribed but autonomous prerogatives nevertheless operate under an overarching rule system (Ostrom 2010).

The diverse nature of the SDGs requires that governance cannot only be treated as a goal, whether stand-alone or embedded within individual goals, but as transcending existing mechanisms. Governance will need to be a careful political process built around broad-based consensus and collective legitimacy, in order to optimise the delivery of goals. Effective governance systems that deliver all of the SDGs should address the complex interactions outlined above, achieving synergy where goals may interact positively, and resolving conflicts where they may interact negatively.

The framework proposed above helps clarify how and where the SDGs face particular governance challenges. Differences and similarities of governance challenges and opportunities correspond to their placement in our conceptual framework. Overall, the challenge is about adopting and adapting existing institutional structures and socio-political conditions, as well as engaging entirely new mechanisms, stakeholders, and perspectives.

Inner-level goals focused on individual and collective outcomes have similar governance and institutional structures, stemming predominantly from the historical role of the state in relation to the provision of health, education, and welfare, the initiatives of the 1990s, and the experience with the MDGs. Whilst the formal institutional structures may be in place, many developing countries will require continued support to strengthen structures and institutions for inner-level goals in order to govern effectively.

At this inner level, the alignment of comparable goals and their implementation across many of these sectors points to broadly synergistic governance opportunities. However, such alignment is often far from politically feasible; it is strongly dependent upon transforming existing social norms and conditions, such as gender inequalities in the public and private spheres, which are entrenched by political and economic relations and will require change over generations.

Moreover, at the inner level, there exists the challenge of connecting the public and the private, which relates to many features in, for example, the gender goal (Goal 5), the education goal (Goal 4) on appreciating cultural diversity, and the poverty goal (Goal 1) on building the resilience of the poor. The issue here is how the state and the market negotiate with the realm of the family, the emotional, and the cultural.

For example, providing information for poor, young women about reproductive rights and enhancing access to contraception requires engaging with young girls, boys, families, communities, faith-based organisations, and schools to better understand adolescent sexuality, gender identities, and relationships, and building supportive connections with the health sector. This entails planning, open discussion of difficult issues, and leadership.

In this realm, the non-governmental or 'third sector' can play a pivotal role. In the fields of SRH and gender, NGOs frequently deliver programmes on issues or to groups that the state sector finds problematic (e.g. abortion and adolescent sexual health) and in which the private sector has little commercial interest (e.g. services for poor or excluded minority groups). In the next chapter, this example of inter-goal governance is used to explore a range of possible governance mechanisms. Middle-level, infrastructure-related goals pose particular governance problems relating to conflicts and trade-offs, often between private and public interests, with multiple stakeholders. The middle level represents a relatively new domain for integrated global development goal setting, and brings with it a number of challenges.

This level is where much of the global economy is concentrated, and typically decisions are taken by a small number of powerful actors across both the public and private sectors, by elites, and by technical experts on behalf of the wider public.[9] The combination of private interests and weaker accountability mechanisms mean decisions are typically made without consideration of the potential interactions with the inner or outer levels. There is an endemic lack of transparency and accountability to the public and, in the SDGs process, little attention is given to local government and organised local communities.

In addition, over the past few decades there has been a positive normativity around building infrastructure associated with energy, water provision, urban development, and growth as ends in themselves. In many countries this is

---

[9] Whilst most people have first-hand experience of service delivery at the inner-level, associated for example with attending school or receiving healthcare, few have experienced or have knowledge of the decision-making processes, implementation, or delivery of services at the middle level. The goals at this level are typically removed from individual experiences.

associated with widening inequalities, problems of environmental sustainability, and intergenerational inequity. Our framework reiterates the importance of interrogating how infrastructure interacts with other levels, and how this can be governed.

The outer level comprises goals relating to land, sea, air, and biodiversity. The governance and management of each of these raises unique challenges. This level currently has the most fragmented governance and institutional landscape, often involving non-binding international agreements and conventions (e.g. the Convention on Biological Diversity (CBD) and the United Nations Framework Convention on Climate Change (UNFCCC)). Outer-level goal governance is currently weak, and its structures consist largely of monitoring and convening processes only, while incentives for stronger governance at this level are poor. Furthermore, current governance structures are focused on environmental conservation, and do not clearly connect to the objectives of well-being in the inner-level goals.

Goals relating to global public goods and shared common resources represent significant challenges, as they rely on greater levels of cooperation and investment in sectors in which the outputs/rewards are less obviously apparent to the electorate in any single country and/or are over longer time horizons; often a generation or more, and certainly beyond an electoral cycle.

Drawing together the above observations, we conclude that the nature of governance challenges changes as you move outwards from the centre of the framework and its well-being goals. For goals in the inner level, many government instruments already exist for delivery, even if they do not always work efficiently or equitably. As we move outward, these mechanisms disintegrate, conflicts arise, and soft laws prevail. As with interactions between goals, potential governance systems are more likely to be similar between goals operating within the same level. The challenge of governing within levels is about building new relationships and new mechanisms that overcome sectoral and ministerial silos.

On the other hand, the interactions occurring between goals that fall into different levels are markedly more complex, and correspondingly, raise more complex governance challenges. This is a key point revealed by our framework, and remains to be addressed if the goals are to be effectively achieved. The challenge of governing across levels is likely to require innovative forms of collective consensus-building, with the inclusion and participation of new stakeholders, across scales, and across sectors.

The significance of the infrastructure level

In the context of rapid urbanisation, population growth, climate change, and diminishing resources, the middle, infrastructural level goals represent simultaneously the greatest challenge and the greatest opportunity to achieve the sustainable development agenda. In this, the most neglected level in terms of the academic and policy discourse, we find the greatest potential synergies, not only between goals within the level, but also the greatest leverage to positively influence the achievement of goals across levels.

The goals of the outer, environmental level can be achieved only if the middle level is governed effectively. The current approach of attempting to govern the outer level without addressing the middle level has meant that the burden placed on global governance initiatives at the outer level is too great. Outer-level goals also function as the ultimate arbitration on the success or failure of the SDGs in terms of sustainability. Inner-level goals will more likely be achieved at the expense of the outer-level goals until resources are virtually exhausted, ecological tipping points are reached, and ecosystem resilience breached. Whilst monitoring and recording of global scale ecosystems will be necessary to ensure that there really is global sustainability, our analysis suggests that the intractable problems of managing the global environment for the benefit of people can be neatly sidestepped by focusing sustainability targets within middle-level goals.

There is a risk that efforts to achieve middle-level goals will be prone to domination by strong special interest groups and short-termism, and will revert to current centralised public and private governance structures and 'business as usual' approaches. Historically, this is the domain of the technical 'experts', where decisions are made on people's behalf. For these reasons, good governance of goals in the middle level requires the strengthening of local government and for decisions to be brought into the realm of public, democratic debate. The significance of the middle level in terms of its interactions with the inner and outer levels means that decisions ought not to be taken by an unaccountable few. Broad-based consensus based on legitimate political procedures of all concerned parties will be vital for the viability of the SDGs agenda.

Recommendations

Our analysis leads to a number of specific recommendations for governments in the development of governance structures for the proposed SDGs. Firstly, we urge governments to: devise formal governance mechanisms at the national and sub-national levels that are characterised by deliberation, participation, and transparency in decision-making; engage community organisations who are already mobilised around these issues; and invite democratic debate around middle-level goals and particularly conflicts. Responsibilities should be defined, accountability systems put in place, and human capacities built accordingly.

Secondly, we suggest that it is important to learn from and build upon existing governance mechanisms and institutional arrangements. There are several models in existence that are at least partially successful in international standard setting, which might provide useful mechanisms for such governance, such as the UN-REDD for forest resources management and the International Organisation for Standardisation (ISO) for standards of health and environmental protection. We illustrate some of these in the next chapter.

Finally, the particular focus of governance and international support by donors should be towards developing the capacity of institutions to operate at the middle, infrastructural level of goals, and to manage, regulate, and govern decision-making and development there.

More generally, we suggest that the diverse nature of the SDGs requires that governance cannot be treated as a goal itself (United Nations High-Level Panel of Eminent Persons on the Post-2015 Development Agenda 2012) or embedded within individual goals (Foresti 2014), but needs to be a careful political process by which the collective delivery of goals at different levels is optimised, providing the necessary broad-based consensus and collective legitimacy required to optimise their delivery. Effective governance systems that deliver all of the SDGs should address the complex interactions outlined above, achieving synergy where goals may interact positively, and resolving conflicts where they may interact negatively.

References

Baker, A., Hudson, D., and Woodward, R. (2005). 'Introduction', in Baker, A., Hudson, D., and Woodward, R. (eds) *Governing Financial Globalisation: International Political Economy and Multi-Level Governance*, London: Routledge.

Foresti, M. (2014, February 5). 3 reasons 'governance' should not only be a stand-alone development goal. *The Interpreter.* Retrieved from http://www.lowyinterpreter.org/post/2014/02/05/3-reasons-governance-should-not-be-a-stand-alone-development-goal.aspx?COLLCC=602054812&

Hulme, D. (2013). The Post-2015 development agenda: learning from the MDGs. Southern Voice Occasional Paper 2. Dhaka, Bangladesh: Centre for Policy Dialogue.

Open Working Group of the General Assembly on Sustainable Development Goals. (2014). Open Working Group proposal for Sustainable Development Goals document A/68/970. New York: United Nations. Retrieved from http://undocs.org/A/68/970

Ostrom, B. (2010). Beyond Markets and States: Polycentric Governance of Complex Economic Systems. *American Economic Review, 100* (June 2010), 1–33.

United Nations High-Level Panel. (2012). Realising the future we want for all: report to the Secretary General. New York: United Nations.

Waage, J., Banerji, R, Campbell, O, Chirwa, E, Collender, G, Dieltiens, V, Dorward, A, et al (2010). 'The Millennium Development Goals: a cross-sectoral analysis and principles for goal setting after 2015' *The Lancet*, vol 376, no. 9745,   991-1023. DOI: http://dx.doi.org/10.1016/S0140-6736(10)61196-8

Case study on sexual and reproductive health and education: reflections on interlinkage and governance

Susannah H. Mayhew[*], Elaine Unterhalter[†],
Nigel Poole[‡], Niheer Dasandi[§], Niall Winters[ˤ]
and on behalf of the Health and Education
Cluster, UCL-LIDC: Thinking Beyond Sectors for
Sustainable Development

[*]London School of Hygiene and Tropical Medicine, Department of Global Health and Development, [†]University College London Institute of Education, Department of Humanities and Social Sciences, [‡]School of Oriental and African Studies, Centre for Environment, Development and Policy, [§]University College London, School of Public Policy, [ˤ]University of Oxford, Department of Education

Introduction

In this chapter, we select several SDGs on health (SDG 3), education (SDG 4), and gender (SDG 5), and explore their interactions and the challenges this poses for their governance. In the previous chapter, we proposed that these specific goals shared, with some others, a focus on individual and population well-being, and are supported in this by goals which provide the infrastructure and services (e.g. food, energy, and employment) to achieve this, and ultimately by other goals which provide the environmental resources necessary to infrastructure

How to cite this book chapter:
Mayhew, S. H, Unterhalter, E, Poole, N, Dasandi, N, and Winters, N. 2015.
  Case study on sexual and reproductive health and education: reflections on
  interlinkage and governance. In: Waage, J and Yap, C. (eds.) *Thinking Beyond Sectors for Sustainable Development.* Pp. 89–107. London: Ubiquity Press. DOI: http://dx.doi.org/10.5334/bao.i

and services. We also suggested that, as well-being goals, they have similarities in their governance and institutional structure relating to the historical role of the state in the provision of health and education, and the experience of past international initiatives, particularly the MDGs.

However, we observed that such similarities do not mean that the important links between these goals are easily recognised or governed. In this chapter, we will first present the evidence for important interactions between these goals, and then explore the barriers to their integration, and particularly the problems for governance. Finally, we will explore a number of possible models for governing these interactions.

The reader may want to refer back to chapters in the first part of this book on human health, population growth, and education, information and knowledge, for an insight into the evolution of these different sectors and their goal-setting processes, and to the previous chapter for the conceptual framework on the interactions and governance of the SDGs mentioned above. Finally, while we examine here a specific interaction between only three goals, we seek to illustrate the more general challenges and opportunities for the governance of SDGs and their interactions.

There are many important interactions between interventions in health, education, and gender, but we have selected a particularly significant one for our examination here, the relationship between SRH and education, particularly of young women.

Interactions between sexual and reproductive health and education and their governance challenges

The interactions between SRH and education are associated both with an interconnection of effects and with processes, intrinsic to each, where the one draws on the other. Demographic and Health Surveys data in many countries show correlation between the uptake of primary education (as measured by enrolment, attendance, and completion) and uptake of SRH services, leading to better outcomes, particularly reduced maternal mortality, better neonatal survival, better sexual health outcomes, greater women's autonomy over decision-making regarding health, and possibly household economics and family redistribution of esteem and influence for women. Thus, through this connection with sexual and reproductive health, we can see a link between girls' schooling and some gender and women's rights goals, as articulated in the Beijing Declaration, the MDGs, and other similar international declarations and agreements.

In trying to understand the interaction between SRH and primary education, we think it is useful to separate out effects as follows: first, that part of the interaction that is noted through impact evaluations; and second, the part of the interaction that is associated with processes, which needs some further investigation (the research base on this is not yet so strong). It appears that processes that facilitate the interaction include flows of information and resources, actions of inclusion, and the conferring of esteem. Thus it may be that even being in a position to attend and remain at school, whether or not one formally gains a qualification, or the capacity to read information leaflets, e.g. on contraception, bestows status in a society/community, which is in itself important in securing SRH outcomes.

There are some important gaps in our knowledge: we do not know whether the content of the education, the pedagogy, and how it is organised, have any bearing on SRH outcomes. It appears that generic education is important, but this may be because research has not dug deep enough, and we have not yet teased out the features of which aspects of education are important. Although we see the relationship between schooling and improved SRH outcomes across many different country settings and different kinds of locales, we still do not know the causal relationship or what the 'trigger' process is (and whether it lies in the education system or somewhere else). But we do know that the line of travel goes from what happens to a child to what is done as an adult. However, data on effects of lessons regarding SRH given in school on outcomes later in life are very inconclusive, and much of this research has been conducted specifically in response to the HIV epidemic in sub-Saharan Africa (e.g. Doyle et al. 2010).

Governance concerns show some of the dynamics of school-linked solutions to resistance to classroom teaching on SRH. In most countries there is large-scale public sector provision for schooling, although private sector provision is increasing in significance, and there is some public-private partnership; however this will always be a junior partner to public sector provision. By contrast maternal health provision is a mix of public and private sector provision. It is largely private in Asia, there is an emerging private (for-profit) sector in Africa, and some NGO (not-for-profit, including Church-based) provision. In virtually all countries, neonatal health and family planning fall largely into the realm of state provision, unless women deliver in a private health facility. Child immunisation and welfare are generally distributed through the public sector worldwide. Family planning, while also widespread in the public sector, is increasingly distributed through pharmacies (condoms, pills, and emergency contraception). Intrauterine devices, implants, and sterilisation are provided in clinics (mostly public and NGO). Social marketing (subsidised provision, usually through pharmacies) is also important for the distribution of family planning, representing public endorsement for private delivery. This sketch indicates that the big picture framing the interactions between these two fields is largely about public governance, provision and regulation of schooling, and child immunisation and welfare, which branches or morphs into a mix of public-private engagement around SRH for adults (there are some parallels with a wider provision of education for adults).

International Human Rights agreements, governing actions of both public and private actors, help to frame interactions between these sectors. The International Convention on the Rights of the Child (entered into force in 1990 after global ratification) protects the child's right to the highest attainable standard of health and to education. Protection of SRHR is more difficult, frequently being seen as a socially or culturally defined right, but the declarations and platforms of action from both the 1994 ICPD and 1995 United Nations Conference on Women in Beijing, explicitly link SRH rights to existing human rights detailed under the International Covenant on Economic, Social and Cultural Rights (entered into force 1976). Rights frameworks tend to govern much NGO and public sector work, but the growth of the private sectors in both health and education has created something of a social market, where rights are framed increasingly as 'consumer choices'.

The regulation of the private, for-profit sector in health is very difficult. The relationship of the private for-profit sector with governments is unclear, although governments (States Parties) ultimately have responsibility under international human rights frameworks for the actions of private sector actors under their jurisdiction. Private professional groups (e.g. medical associations) can be very powerful when it comes to influencing policy decisions on health issues: big pharmaceutical companies are extremely powerful lobbyists on policy decision-making, particularly where their interests (e.g. on drugs procurement or licensing) are at stake.

We see something similar in education, where the NGO sector is more in conversation with the public sector, while the private for-profit sector is more autonomous or connects through financial flows and the power of edubusiness (i.e. multinational companies like Pearson PLC which make profits out of selling key components of the education system like the software for conducting standardised tests, textbooks, and so forth). This profit motive is particularly evident in the areas of electronic-based education (elearning), and increasingly in mobile and electronic health (mHealth/eHealth). Often the approach is to highlight problems with educational systems and teachers' practices, and to frame this as a 'crisis' that can be used primarily by the corporate sector as a key rationale to develop parallel and costly systems. These systems are underpinned by the latest technologies (often mobile technologies). While technical innovation is welcome, in many cases is it not adequately supported by real efforts to understand and address the weaknesses identified in educational systems. The crisis thus becomes self-perpetuating: teachers' professional practice comes under continuous questioning, and the weakness of educational systems is highlighted over and over again. However, if education is to be a priority, any proposed technology-based interventions must be seen to work with existing systems in an equitable manner, and seek to improve educational opportunity for all, especially those at the margins of society.

Governance of the NGO sector is somewhat easier, since NGOs often have a commitment to working with governments. They play an important role in helping communities to engage with, and accept SRH education through both the education and health sectors. They have often been important in supporting schools to take forward SRH initiatives through girls' clubs, for example, and specialist training for teachers. One particularly successful example, the multi-donor funded flagship Geração Biz programme in Mozambique (see **Box 1**),

---

Box. 1 Experience of a multi-agency Adolescent SRHR programme in Mozambique

The programme is implemented by an international NGO in collaboration with three ministries: Health, Education and Gender/Youth and Sport and support from UNFPA. The Scandinavian countries and Holland support the programme and plans for going to scale are developed. The International NGOs Pathfinder and IPPF are involved in the training.

The PGB (Programa Geração Biz) started in 1999 as a multi-sectoral/multi-component pilot project implemented in two provinces. The PGB was gradually scaled up to cover 11 provinces and more than 80 per cent of the districts. From the pilot phase in 1999 up to 2004, the objective of PGB was 'To improve ASRH, increase gender awareness, reduce the incidence of unplanned pregnancies, and decrease young people's vulnerability to STIs, HIV, and unsafe abortion'. From 2004, a rights-based approach was adopted and youth participation enhanced. A new objective, expected results, and guiding principles were developed. The objective of the PGB from 2005 to the present is 'To improve ASRH, including a reduction in the incidence of early or unwanted pregnancy, STIs and HIV, through activities that equip young people with the knowledge, skills, and services needed for positive behaviour change' (Country Study Report 2014).

PGB is structured around three main and interlinked components:

  i) Youth-friendly clinical services under the responsibility the School and Adolescent Health Section of the Ministry of Health;
 ii) In school interventions coordinated by the Department of Special Programmes of the Ministry of Education and implemented by schools; and
iii) Community outreach targeting out-of-school youths coordinated by the National Directorate of Youth of the Ministry of Youth and Sports, and implemented by youth associations.

A 2004 evaluation was positive and recommended that the programme should scale up to cover the whole of Mozambique. Around 2010 donors took the decision to pull out. Adequate alternatives to donor funding were not secured and host-ministry capacities were low, so the programme had largely collapsed by 2014.

involved collaboration between NGO and public sectors, including the Ministries of Health, Education, and Youth and Sports, to support community youth groups, develop teaching and information materials, train school teachers in facilitating SRHR knowledge to schoolchildren, and train/equip health staff to meet young people's needs for SRHR services. Lack of sustainable funding proved its downfall.

Over and above some of the dynamics of governance, the history of the link between international goals in education and SRH is important, and has a bearing on how we can understand the interactions. Historically, since the 1960s the promotion of the education of girls and women was associated with initiatives in what was then termed 'family planning'. Later this came to be displaced by increased focus on economics, citizenship, or gender equality. There are institutional links between UNFPA, UNICEF, and UNESCO, as part of the United Nations 'family', but there are also rivalries and the governance structures of these organisations affects how they frame issues; for example, UNESCO is governed by country representation, like the United Nations, while UNICEF accepts private donations, and has been adept at establishing particular kinds of niches. UNFPA was formerly a programme under the UNDP and remains co-located in many countries; like UNESCO it is governed by United Nations member states (12 donors and 24 programme countries). Compared to UNICEF, it has a tiny budget (mostly funded by donor states), and therefore cannot implement programmes; there is sometimes tension between the two over maternal health mandates, though family planning remains the preserve of UNFPA.

The framing of the MDGs, and some of the direction taken by the EFA movement have been associated with something short of trade-offs, more like stumbles, which have made realising the links with SRH more difficult; notably a lack of attention to safety in schools, particularly SRGBV, inadequate opportunities for women's literacy, and access to lifelong learning, which would entail, for example, knowing a mainstream language or being able to attend some kind of discussion group. These gaps have negative consequences for SRH. Moreover, many of the ways in which EFA has been addressed has promoted a human capital approach to education, rather than one with a strong social justice ethos. Thus, currently there is a keen interest in how technology can be used in education to prepare populations for the 'knowledge economy', and in particular, how solutions can be aligned to business needs and the development of life skills. However, in working with marginalised communities there will be a greater need for 'social arrangements that permit all to participate as peers in social life. Overcoming injustice means dismantling institutionalised obstacles that prevent some people from participating on a par with others as full partners in social interaction' (Fraser 2008: 16, cited in Tikly & Barrett, 2011: 6). According to Tikly (2011), Fraser's work is very significant in that she draws attention to 'three dimensions of social justice' (Tikly & Barrett, 2011: 6), which we reframe here to investigate the role of technology in relation to both education and health:

- Redistribution: Does everyone have access to technology?
- Recognition: Understanding the processes underpinning the marginalisation of particular social excluded groups (e.g. rural girls, nomadic communities, refugees, and indigenous groups). Does the development of new technologies have unintended consequences that could result in continuing to support marginalisation, even indirectly?
- Participation: How can marginalised groups have a voice in any decision-making processes that affect their lives? What is the role of technology in supporting this process? How can marginalised groups have a role in the design/rollout of new technologies?

The 2nd June 2013 draft outline of the Open Working Group for Sustainable Development Goals explicitly drew a connection between SRH and education that had been disconnected in previous policy frameworks in their framing of Goals 3, 4, and 5. However, the dominant attention to the interactions in terms of effects, rather than processes, means that the ways to realise these connections are not well understood, and the institutional, organisational, and research undergirding needs to be put in place. The highly politicised nature of SRH was underscored in the negotiations culminating in Revision 1 of the Zero Draft, which saw the removal of the sub-goal for universal access to SRHR from the health Goal and qualified under the gender Goal; a significantly weaker position that risks governments being able to ignore the more difficult SRH issues, such as safe abortion, adolescent contraception, and so forth, because they are no longer a target for the health goal, nor are they seen as a core remit for the gender goal. This was the subject of intense negotiation, with SRHR NGOs lobbying all sympathetic European delegations as well as African and Asian governments, to get them to call for the reinstatement of universal SRHR under the health goal in the final round (13th Session) of the Open Working Group negotiations in July. Universal access to SRHR was successfully reinstated under the health Goal, but it remains to be seen whether it will be retained in the final document to be agreed by the States Parties in June 2015.

Analysing the challenges to governing the interactions

Power — One way to think about governing interactions links with the public/private melange in education and SRH discussed above. Education is dominated by the public sector because of a strong association with the legitimation of existing regimes (as schooling is often a key issue in elections, both national and local), publicity around politicians, the formulation of a national identity, perceptions about economic achievement, and so forth. As a sector, education is very visible and associated with particular forms of accountability, symbols, and ideas about appropriate distribution. SRH can also be highly political, as noted earlier, but the pathways associated with this tend to be more moral and religious (e.g. on issues such as access to safe abortion, adolescent contraception, and rights for sexual minorities). Although these are highly politicised, they are not so much seen as issues of accountability or drivers of narratives of economic progress. They are unlikely to be linked to charges of corruption or views on how governments construct budgets, but are invoked around symbolic, national, or religious identities which can be very powerful, as well as arguments of gender-equity and the status of women, which have importance for certain types of foreign aid. Maternal and neonatal mortalities tend not to be election issues.

A second way to think about power is to consider individual power. In SRH discussions, women's autonomy is seen as a means and an end, and this is also a feature of the policy discussions in education. Which part of this continuum is stressed tends to be associated with the position of who is talking. Some of the conceptual knitting of ideas, empowerment, and inter-sectionality has been formulated in each sector and then critiqued, but the connection between them has not been much worked up analytically or empirically.

Global framings — initially the population control/sustainability argument drove much discourse on development in the 1950s and 1960s (at this time education was largely about primary provision and adult literacy). In the 1980s in SRH, NGOs and women's rights groups took a different path, culminating in the ICPD in 1994 and the shift from population control to women's sexual and reproductive rights, bodily autonomy, and so forth. In education in the late 1980s, there was a period of struggle between UNESCO, UNICEF, and World Bank over structural adjustment and whether it can have a human face, i.e. big or small state, and what kind of role there can be for the market and the community. This was resolved in 1990 with the EFA movement identifying education needs and rights as the conceptual glue that can hold together quite different framings of what the global landscape is or should be. The MDGs with a goal on maternal health provide a mechanism for NGOs and civil society groups to hold governments to account. This movement does not link up at all with the EFA movement, nor with the ICPD (which delinked population from development). The MDGs focus on UPE separates out the connection with maternal health, and means that different NGO or citizen collations are holding different sections of government or the global machinery to account. The 2000 period is one of parallel initiatives and attempts to start to reconnect, but it is quite fragile, and very much a plaything of the aid fashions and donor power (Mayhew & Adjei 2004; Unterhalter 2014).

Ideas — In the 1960s, education and population control were both seen as pathways to economic growth. Neither was framed in terms of autonomy, individual rights, citizenship, or inclusion. Today, other than discussions of correlation, very few ideas link education and SRH together. Institutionally they are taught in separate schools, handled by different departments, and debated at different conferences. Delinking population and health does not help, but some of the conceptual knitting ideas (empowerment and intersectionality) have begun to take forward connections, however these have stalled. In relation to discussions of population, this is a difficult topic to broach because of historical associations of population discussion with forced sterilisation, coercion, and fears of eugenics (from past policies in India, China, and Nazi Germany). This has made it very difficult to take forward any discussion of population linked to rights, even within the health community (Newman et al. 2014).

In education the way the field of ideas has developed has been through turning inwards to a concern with learning and quality, a focus on pedagogy and management, but not on the links with other sectors, except in broad brushstrokes or taken as obvious givens. For example, there are ubiquitous depictions along the lines of 'if you educate a girl... you solve every development problem' (Monkman & Hoffman 2013; Unterhalter 2015, in press). The history of the ideas in the field indicate parallel discourses to those in SRH aiming in the same direction (individual rights and women's equity for improved development), but are not very clear on how to get there together, with no exploration of what needs to link up with what/who and why/how?

We thus have two very powerful sectors, which claim to be public goods and to constitute the moral underpinning of all other development goals. Each wants to retain its own territory, bureaucratic machineries, and technologies. In the health sector the power of doctors is notable; in the education sector there is considerable power of the higher education sector and political parties' machineries. In both cases these are groupings with hydraulic influence. In Ghana, for example, there has been a devolution of a lot of social development to local government. But there has been no decentralisation in health and in education this has been uneven (S. H. Mayhew, personal communications 2013). Although there are proposals for decentralisation, there is great resistance to change, and officials at a local level merely carry out decisions taken far away in the capital. In South Africa, where education and hospitals were devolved to provinces as part of the constitutional settlement in 1994, this is seen as raising many difficult issues about management and concerns about efficiency and delivery. In the face of this, application is sometimes made to the private sector to come in and 'make good'.

Critical junctures

Clearly there are many critical junctures for these two fields, and the SDGs provide an opportunity to both raise awareness of them and move towards realising actions to enhance them. There is an attenuated engagement

between education, women, and health, but with very few substantive connections around programming, policy, and practice. There is much to do.
Forecasting of population and its distribution (migration, urbanisation,
and so forth) is not very well done in either the health or education sectors,
although it is well used by the private sector wanting to know the nature and
location of their future markets. Demographics is not seen as an accountability issue. The women's movement and the education community need
to re-engage. The coalition of women's groups and SRH health activists that
negotiated the Cairo agreement was not sustained, but could reconnect. In
education, the links with the women's movement would need to be built from
the beginning.

Potential solutions and their implementation

As the previous chapter argued, the diversity of the SDGs requires new thinking about governance and mechanisms that transcend existing governance
mechanisms. In the concentric circles model presented there, health and
education goals fall in the inner circle (individual and collective outcomes).
These are well-established components of government policies worldwide
and can be naturally synergistic, as the connections between education and
SRH outcomes discussed in this chapter serve to illustrate. There are well-
established governance mechanisms for these goals but, as this chapter has
also shown, there are nevertheless many governance challenges; particularly
in the context of the promotion of private-sector technologies and exten-
sion of market economy principles into what has traditionally been public
sector territory, which is changing the public-private mix of the governance
landscape.

The conceptual framework introduced in the last chapter also illustrates the
interactions between levels of goals: inner- and middle-level (infrastructural)
goals are seen as reciprocal, e.g. reliable, resilient infrastructure and energy are
necessary to deliver health and education services, while an educated, healthy
labour force is necessary for promotion of sustainable economic growth. The
outer-level goals (environment and underlying support systems) are seen as
the goals underpinning sustainable development, though there are specific
interconnections with the inner-level goals. For example, population dynamics (growth, migration, and urbanisation) are influenced by availability and
acceptability of contraceptive services, delivered by public and private health
infrastructures as well as education (as described in this chapter). Population
dynamics also have direct and indirect effects on climate and environmental
change. Governance systems need to be able to address such complex interactions. The previous chapter on Governing Sustainable Development Goals
argues that interactions between goals at the same level (as between health/SRH
and education) are theoretically more governable, and the greatest governance

challenge (which will have an effect on the achievement of all levels of SDGs) is governance of the middle-level infrastructural goals.

In this final section we explore possible solutions to the complexities facing the governance of SDGs interactions. Stakeholders are key to resolving the governance challenges associated with which targets come under which goals. The final position of the targets under set goals will influence which stakeholders are considered primary actors and who they are likely to interact with. We first consider who the main stakeholders are for governing interactions between health and education sectors under two different final-target scenarios. Both health and education sectors are characterised by strong and independent governance structures that potentially make it hard to govern across them. Second, we therefore explore how institutional silos that currently create barriers to effective, synergistic governance might be broken down.

Stakeholders

The deletion, in the penultimate draft of the SDGs, of the SRH target from the health goal and its repositioning under the gender goal quite significantly changed the potential and primary stakeholders (see **Table 1** below). Although it was reinstated under the health goal in the final draft,[10] it could still be lost during the year-long intergovernmental discussions that began in November 2014. If it is, the attainment of universal access to SRHR will be under threat, and the contribution of the education sector in helping to attain SRHR goals could become much more significant. Typically, ministries of health would be expected to lead on attainment of the SRHR target, but sensitive elements within it (especially access to safe abortion services, adolescent contraception, and rights of sexual minorities) remain controversial and opposed by many governments. Moving the SRHR target under the gender goal deflects responsibility from the health sector to a much weaker ministry (gender or women's affairs), requiring a much greater effort on the part of dedicated stakeholders and advocates to ensure their efforts are seen as legitimate activities for the health sector targets (which would not include this goal). This will not be a problem in countries whose governments are committed to upholding SRHR rights as defined in Cairo and Beijing, but it will be a significant barrier to effective implementation of SRHR in countries whose governments roundly oppose the full SRHR agenda.

Historically, links between ministries of health and ministries of education are weak (although there are similarities between these two powerful sectors, as noted earlier). It may be that in Scenario 2 in **Table 1** there is an opportunity and a need for ministries of education to play a key role

---

[10] As of April 2015.

in helping to achieve the SRHR target, through stepping up its efforts at school-based SRHR education and school-based health care (including contraception). In the long-term, if ministries of education can prioritise attainment of target 4.2 (ensuring all girls and boys complete quality primary education), this would have a significant impact on improving the uptake of contraceptives over a generation, which would itself lead to a significant improvement in the main SRHR goals, providing access to a choice of family planning methods.

	Scenario 1: Retaining 'Universal access to SRHR' within Goal 4 (Health)	Scenario 2: 'Universal access to SRHR' appears only in the Goal 5 (Gender)
Primary Stakeholders	• Ministries of health • Public health services (managers, providers) • NGOs and their service providers • Private for-profit providers • Professional medical associations	• Ministries of women's affairs/gender • Women's rights NGOs
Secondary Stakeholders	• Ministries of education • Ministries of youth/sport • Ministries of women/gender • UN/IGOs working on women's health issues in particular • Health sector donors • SRHR advocacy NGOs/CSOs • Ministries of finance (usually hold budget lines for commodities procurement)	• Ministries of health • Ministries of education • Ministries of youth/sport • UN/IGOs working on women's health issues in particular • SRHR advocacy NGOs/CSOs (may still wish to be involved in promoting SRHR) • Health sector donors (may still wish to be involved in promoting SRHR)
Other Stakeholders	• Women's rights NGOs	• Health service providers (public, NGO, and private) will only be seen as stakeholders if target 5.6 is pursued by ministries of health (although some NGOs and possibly private providers may pursue elements of the target unilaterally). • Ministries of finance (usually hold budget lines for commodities procurement)

(Contd.)

	Scenario 1: Retaining 'Universal access to SRHR' within Goal 4 (Health)	Scenario 2: 'Universal access to SRHR' appears only in the Goal 5 (Gender)
Risks	Controversial elements (safe abortion; adolescent family planning and sexuality education; and right to education, information, and services for sexual minorities) are downplayed by ministries of health, but it will be difficult to ignore them entirely.	Without ministries of health acting as lead stakeholders it is much easier for governments to ignore sensitive SRHR issues entirely. Ministries of gender/ women (note how the two are often used synonymously) are typically very weak ministries; there are occasional exceptions, but it largely depends on leadership and the extent to which that leadership has the ear of other powerful ministers/leaders. Health has not typically been regarded as a core mandate for gender and equality actions, so making a new set of alliances, including with health, youth, and education ministries, will take considerable time and effort.

Table 1: Key stakeholders for governance of linkages between sexual and reproductive health and education in two Sustainable Development Goals scenarios.

CSO, civil society organisation; IGO, inter-governmental organisation; NGO, non-governmental organisation; SRHR, sexual and reproductive health and rights; UN, United Nations.

Once the final placement of targets is confirmed, it will be clear who the primary stakeholders should be for each goal and target. However, given all the possible multiple interactions between the SGDs, it is unclear who will, or should be tasked with acting on adapting or establishing the structures and mechanisms to govern these interactions.

How can institutional silos be tackled?

Conducting development work in governmental or institutional silos is nothing new, and in the health sector it has been debated for nearly half a century in terms of whether, at what level, and which programmes should be aligned or integrated to form 'holistic' care versus being provided separately or 'selectively'. There are still no clear criteria for achieving integrated care even for packages of services within the most clearly related areas (e.g. linking HIV and other SRH services or the 'integrated management of childhood illnesses') (WHO 2015). Breaking down silos between entire sectors is significantly harder, and requires considerable and sustained effort by strong leaders of the different sectors, particularly where there is no consensus on whose responsibility it should be to oversee progress on sensitive targets.

While resource allocation for inter-sectoral work through budgetary processes in, for example, a ministry of finance or national planning commission will take place at the highest national executive level, assigning responsibility for cross-cutting activities requires coordination at the level of separate national ministries. For example, there are studies from Mozambique of successful interlinkages between ministries at a programme level, where a range of government, NGO, and donor actors have come together within a clearly demarcated and supported governance structure, shared between relevant ministries on a rotating basis, but sustaining those interlinkages without strong leadership and adequate financing is problematic (see **Box 1** on the Geração Biz programme). A number of characteristics of successful national governance initiatives can also be distilled from political reform literature, notably Grindle's work on education reforms in South America (Grindle 2004):

- Leadership is critical: to appoint/work for or with other leaders who give strategic support, seize windows of opportunity when they arise, marginalise opponents, and frame the issues to gain strategic support (see **Box 2** on Indian economic reforms);

Box. 2 Key characteristics of Indian economic reforms in 1980s–90s

The executive leaders set the terms of debates about economic reform in the country. Prime Minister Rajiv Gandhi, under whose leadership the reforms were initiated, was careful to avoid framing the debate along ideological lines. Instead, he emphasised the changing nature of the global economy, and the need for a change in policy so that India would not lag behind other countries.

A key role was played by 'the change team', made up of a group of senior bureaucrats and politicians committed to economic reform in the country. The design team consisted of a number of senior bureaucrats who had developed similar ideas about economic reform from having spent time abroad and having been exposed to new economic ideas. The design team went about trying to broaden support for the reforms within various bureaucracies.

His successor, Prime Minister Chandra Shekhar, publicly took a more critical stance towards proposed economic liberalisation to appease voters, while privately encouraging the reform team to be bolder with their proposals.

Source: **Shastri, V.** (1997). The politics of economic liberalisation in India. *Contemporary South Asia*, 6(1), 27–56.

- Establishment of reform teams (with careful thought to composition and placement) able to get on with the job and protected from political debate (see **Box 2** on India), in particular securing safe spaces for debate and planning with a wide range of stakeholders;
- Flexibility of implementation is necessary:
  - Developing a 'problem-driven iterative adaptive approach' (Andrews, Pritchett & Woolcock 2013);
  - Devolution and inter-sectoral planning is probably useful for achieving this.
- Inclusiveness of all key stakeholders is important for achieving buy-in and consensus.

However, governing complex links between health and education in the context of the wider SDGs, which have multiple spheres of interaction at multiple levels, must ultimately go well beyond two or three national sectors to account for the connections to the middle-level infrastructural goals, which are hardest to govern but provide the crucial link across all levels of SDGs.

At an aggregate level, a global institutional architecture with national linkages is probably needed for strategy and policy, especially for handling multi-sectoral goals with synergies, trade-offs, and conflicts, and for monitoring, reporting, and verification of progress. The United Nations agencies provide the most obvious existing global institutional framework, but are fragmented and have struggled to achieve effective cross-sector coordination in the past. Nevertheless, creating new global and national systems and bureaucracies will be unwelcome for many. Appropriate governance can be informed by other existing international collaborations to address specific obligations, targets, or movements in areas other than health and education. These experiences may provide lessons about what does and does not work as governance mechanisms for complex development themes such as the SDGs.

Learning from existing models of inter-sectoral governance

We draw on a number of models or approaches that could be pursued, or at least their principles can provide lessons, to facilitate the political management and governance required to achieve a balance of political leadership, bureaucratic capacity, and the voice and mobilisation of citizens and civil society to pursue legitimate and accountable goals (see chapter 8).

First, a task force is a grouping of diverse individuals or organisations concerned with a theme of common interest, with clearly defined analytical and executive purposes, and with its key attributes being participation, advocacy, focus, and accountability. Accountability for each goal is likely to be located within and through a particular ministry. Leadership can be through an internal or external appointee made by that ministry. The composition of a taskforce would reflect the range of expert stakeholders, likely drawn from the public sector, international organisations, national civil society, and the private sector. One example of a task force approach is that which was used in Zambia in 2007 to analyse and develop opportunities for the acceleration of the commercial utilisation of cassava (Chitundu, Droppelmann & Haggblade 2006). Processes were not entirely smooth, nor outcomes unproblematic, but the approach to multi-stakeholder problem-solving was valuable and replicable (Poole 2010).

A second model for the governance of multi-sectoral and independent players is the cluster approach used by the humanitarian system to improve capacity, predictability, accountability, leadership, and partnership in the coordination of responses to humanitarian needs: 'Clusters provide a clear point of contact and are accountable for adequate and appropriate humanitarian assistance. Clusters create partnerships between international humanitarian actors, national and local authorities, and civil society' (UN OCHA 2015). In the case of such humanitarian work, it is the United Nations Office for the Coordination of Humanitarian Affairs (UN OCHA) that works closely with global and national cluster lead agencies and NGOs to develop policies, coordinate inter-cluster issues, disseminate operational guidance, and organise field support. An acknowledged successful case of cluster coordination is the Nutrition Cluster in Afghanistan. Similarly, significant lessons can be learnt from the global Education Cluster set up by Save the Children and UNICEF (UN ALNAP 2015).

A third is the UN-REDD: the United Nations collaborative initiative on reducing emissions from deforestation and forest degradation in developing countries that bears closest relation to proposed Goal 15 (Protect, restore and promote sustainable use of terrestrial ecosystems, sustainably manage forests, combat desertification, and halt and reverse land degradation and halt biodiversity loss, outer circle), and has synergies with at least proposed Goals 1 (End poverty in all forms everywhere, inner circle) and 2 (End hunger, achieve food security and improved nutrition and promote sustainable agriculture: inner and middle circles), and probably proposed Goal 6 (Ensure availability and sustainable management of water and sanitation for all, cross-cuts all three circles). A convening role and technical expertise are provided by three United Nations organisations: the FAO, the UNDP, and the UNEP. Each is a lead agency for one or more of the work areas. The objective of UN-REDD is to support national processes and promote inclusion of all stakeholders, including indigenous peoples and other forest-dependent communities (UN-REDD 2015). **Figure 3** gives an example of how UN-REDD partners were configured for governance in Paraguay.

The United Nations are not the only type of apex organisation, nor do all models of global governance necessarily share the same principles of coordination, devolution, and accountability. 'Justice for all' specifically appears in proposed Goal 16, but could be considered to underpin other Goals. An existing institution in this field is the International Criminal Court (ICC) at The Hague in the Netherlands. The ICC was founded on the basis of the Rome Statute, which entered into force on 1 July 2002 after ratification by 60 countries, established to help end impunity for the perpetrators of the most serious crimes of concern to the

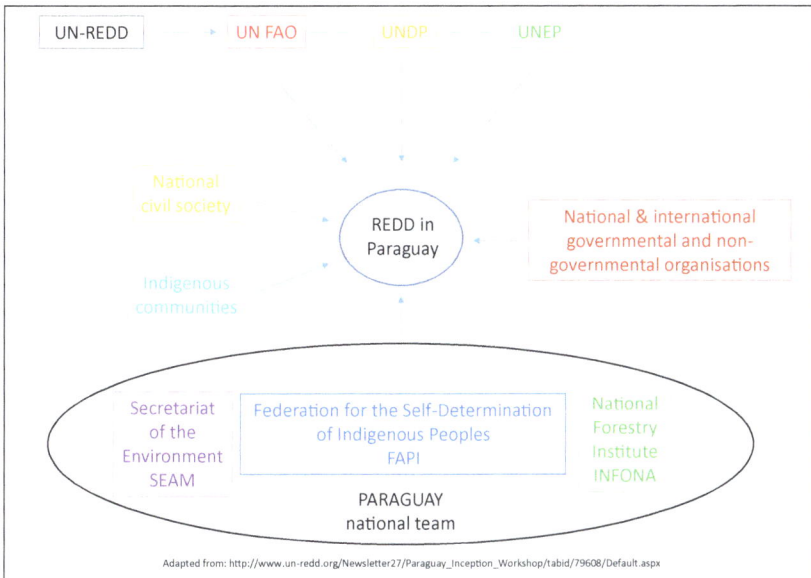

Figure 3: The configuration of the United Nations Collaborative Programme on Reducing Emissions from Deforestation and Forest Degradation partners in Paraguay.

international community (ICC 2015). The ICC is not part of the United Nations system. It is funded primarily by States Parties and also receives voluntary contributions from governments, international organisations, individuals, corporations, and other entities. The limitations in the operation and achievements of the ICC does not invalidate the inter-sectoral and multi-stakeholder model per se. The potential configurations of transnational and multilevel groupings are numerous, and optimal formulations will depend on local circumstances.

Achieving implementation

The models and essential characteristics noted above all have considerable challenges associated with successful implementation. Key among these (again drawing on political reform literature) are as follows: ensuring how any decision-making or governance body goes beyond a talking shop: many interagency taskforces or multi-sector planning/oversight bodies have failed because of a failure to clearly demarcate responsibilities between the different agencies. There must be transparent accountability of such bodies to build trust and confidence in their decisions and actions. The question of where bodies are based is important, and there can be a big difference between the political face and what happens behind the scenes (see **Box 2**).

Overall, the analysis of the challenges of governing the interactions between two inner-circle goals (health, specifically SRH, and education) show that even within inner circle SDGs, there are many complexities facing the development and implementation of successful governance approaches and mechanisms. The complexity increases with the need to additionally govern the interactions between the inner- and middle-level goals (individual and collection outcome, and infrastructure). We have drawn on political science literature and existing examples of multi-sector/multi-agency governance to suggest possible govern-ance models that might be considered by national and international stakehold-ers responsible for implementing the SDGs. Whilst it is clear that governing the interactions between SDGs will be extremely challenging, it is equally clear that the success of the SDGs, both individually and collectively, will depend on effective cross-sector governance mechanisms being established and implemented.

References

Andrews, M., Pritchett, L., Woolcock, M. (2013). Escaping capability traps through Problem Driven Iterative Adaptation (PDIA). *World Develop-ment* Vol 51, November 2013. 234–244. DOI: http://dx.doi.org/10.1016/j. worlddev.2013.05.011

Chitundu, M., Droppelmann, K., & Haggblade, S. (2006). Value chain task force approaches for managing private-public partnerships: Zambia's task for on acceleration of cassava utilisation. Working paper No. 21. Lusaka, Zambia: Food Security Research Project. Retrieved from http://ageconsearch.umn. edu/bitstream/54480/2/wp_21.pdf

Doyle, A. M, Ross, D. A., Maganja, K., Baisley, K., Masesa, C., Andreasen, A., Plummer, M. J., et al. (2010). Long-term biological and behavioural impact of an adolescent sexual health intervention in Tanzania: follow-up survey of the community-based MEMA kwa Vijana Trial. *PLoS Med, 7*(6), e1000287. DOI: http://dx.doi.org/10.1371/journal.pmed.1000287

Fraser, N. (2008). Scales of justice: reimagining political space in a globalising world. Cambridge: Polity Press.

Freeman T., Matsinhe C., Mayhew S.H. for DANIDA (2014). Evaluation of the Danish strategy for the promotion of sexual and reproductive health and rights 2006-2013: Country Study Report: Mozambique: Ministry of Foreign Affairs: Danida, July 2014.

Grindle, M. S. (2004). Despite the odds: the contentious politics of education reform. Princeton, NJ: Princeton University Press.

International Criminal Court (ICC). (2015). *About the court.* Retrieved from http://www.icc-cpi.int/en_menus/icc/about%20the%20court/Pages/ about%20the%20court.aspx

Mayhew S. H., & Adjei S. (2004). Sexual and reproductive health: challenges for priority setting in Ghana's health reforms. *Health Policy and Planning*, *19*(Suppl. 1), 50–61.

Monkman, K., & Hoffman, L. (2013). Girls' education: the power of policy discourse. *Theory and Research in Education, 11.1*(2013), 63–84.

Newman, K., Fisher, S., Mayhew, S., & Stephenson, J. (2014). Population, sexual and reproductive health, rights and sustainable development: forging a common agenda. *Reproductive Health Matters, 22*(43), 53–64. DOI: http://dx.doi.org/10.1016/S0968-8080(14)43770-

Poole, N. D. (2010). Zambia cassava sector policy – recommendations in support of strategy implementation. EU-AAACP Paper Series No. 16. Rome: Food and Agriculture Organization of the United Nations. Retrieved from http://www.euacpcommodities.eu/files/1ESAA01FAO%20AAACP%20Paper%20Series%2016%20Recommendations%20Zambia%20Cassava%20Strat.pdf

Shastri, V. (1997). The politics of economic liberalisation in India. *Contemporary South Asia*, *6*(1), 27–56.

Tikly, L. & Barrett, A. (2011) Social justice, capabilities and the quality of education in low income countries, *International Journal of Educational Development*, 31: 3–14 .

United Nations Active Learning Network for Accountability and Performance in Humanitarian Action (UN ALNAP). (2015). *Review of the global education cluster co-leadership arrangement.* Retrieved from http://www.alnap.org/resource/6354

United Nations collaborative initiative on Reducing Emissions from Deforestation and forest Degradation in developing countries (UN-REDD). (2015). *About the UN-REDD Programme.* Retrieved from http://www.un-redd.org/AboutUN-REDDProgramme/tabid/102613/Default.aspx

United Nations Office for the Coordination of Humanitarian Affairs (UN OCHA). (2015). *Cluster coordination.* Retrieved from http://www.unocha.org/what-we-do/coordination-tools/cluster-coordination

Unterhalter, E. (2014). Measuring education for the Millennium Development Goals: reflections on targets, indicators, and a post-2015 framework. *Journal of Human Development and Capabilities, 15*(1–2), 176–187.

Unterhalter, E. (2015). Gender and education in the global polity. In: K. Mundy, A. Green, B. Lingard, & A. Verger (Eds.), *Handbook of global policy and policy making in education.* London: Wiley-Blackwell, in press.

World Health Organization (WHO). (2015). *Maternal, Newborn, Child and Adolescent Health: Integrated Management of Childhood Illness.* Retrieved from http://www.who.int/maternal_child_adolescent/topics/child/imci/en/

Appendix: Millennium Development Goals and Targets

Goal 1: Eradicate extreme hunger and poverty

Target 1. Halve, between 1990 and 2015, the proportion of people whose income is less than $1.25 a day

Target 2. Halve, between 1990 and 2015, the proportion of people who suffer from hunger

Goal 2: Achieve universal primary education

Target 3. Ensure that, by 2015, children everywhere, boys and girls alike, will be able to complete a full course of primary schooling

Goal 3: Promote gender equality and empower women

Target 4. Eliminate gender disparity in primary and secondary education, preferably by 2005, and in all levels of education no later than 2015

Goal 4: Reduce child mortality

Target 5. Reduce by two-thirds, between 1990 and 2015, the under-five mortality rate

Goal 5: Improve maternal health

Target 6. Reduce by three-quarters, between 1990 and 2015, the maternal mortality ratio

Goal 6: Combat HIV/AIDS, malaria and other diseases

Target 7. Have halted by 2015 and begun to reverse the spread of HIV/AIDS

Target 8. Have halted by 2015 and begun to reverse the incidence of malaria and other major diseases

Goal 7: Ensure environmental sustainability

Target 9. Integrate the principles of sustainable development into country policies and programs and reverse the loss of environmental resources

Target 10. Halve, by 2015, the proportion of people without sustainable access to safe drinking water and basic sanitation

Target 11. Have achieved by 2020 a significant improvement in the lives of at least 100 million slum dwellers

Goal 8: Develop a global partnership for development

Target 12. Develop further an open, rule-based, predictable, nondiscriminatory trading and financial system (includes a commitment to good governance, development, and poverty reduction, both nationally and internationally)

Target 13. Address the special needs of the Least Developed Countries (includes tariff- and quota-free access for Least Developed Countries exports, enhanced program of debt relief for heavily indebted poor countries [HIPCs] and cancellation of official bilateral debt, and more generous official development assistance for countries committed to poverty reduction)

Target 14. Address the special needs of landlocked developing countries and small island developing states (through the Program of Action for the Sustainable Development of Small Island Developing States and 22nd General Assembly provisions)

Target 15. Deal comprehensively with the debt problems of developing countries through national and international measures in order to make debt sustainable in the long term

Target 16. In cooperation with developing countries, develop and implement strategies for decent and productive work for youth

Target 17. In cooperation with pharmaceutical companies, provide access to affordable essential drugs in developing countries

Target 18. In cooperation with the private sector, make available the benefits of new technologies, especially information and communications technologies

Milton Keynes UK
Ingram Content Group UK Ltd.
UKHW020818030923
427740UK00010B/48

9 781909 188426